"Pat Williams reveals secrets learned over a lifetime of leadership in professional sports. From tools for identifying and managing talent to the importance of finding the right collaborators, *The Success Intersection* offers practical advice from some of the most influential people in sports, entertainment, and business. This book is for anyone who wants to compete and succeed at the highest level."

—**Adam Silver**, commissioner of the National Basketball Association

"Pat Williams's new book, *The Success Intersection*, is a powerful, life-changing read!"

—**Bruce Arians**, head coach, Arizona Cardinals

"The books that Pat Williams writes are always thought-provoking and uplifting. *The Success Intersection* is no exception. You'll love reading this one!"

—**Dabo Swinney**, head football coach, Clemson University

"Pat Williams is a book-writing machine with over one hundred books to his credit. His latest work—*The Success Intersection*—is my favorite. After you read this compelling book, I know you will agree with me."

—**Bob Lanier**, NBA legend

"Once I started on *The Success Intersection* by Pat Williams I couldn't stop reading. It's loaded with great information and the stories are terrific. I know you'll be as impacted as I was."

—**Jim McElwain**, head football coach, University of Florida

"*The Success Intersection* really drills down on two areas of maximizing achievement that all coaches strive to develop in their teams—talent and passion. This book provides a clear road map for teams as well as individuals to find their sweet spot in life."

—**Dirk Koetter**, head coach,Tampa Bay Buccaneers

"I have read many of Pat Williams's books and have always benefited. *The Success Intersection* is his best one yet. You'll read it in one sitting."

—**Eric Musselman**, head men's basketball coach, University of Nevada

"Pat Williams's waste-no-time philosophy has informed my work ethic for decades, so I know from experience that he's an authority on this subject. *The Success Intersection* distills all he's learned and put into practice. Pat lays it out in such a way that you can easily intersect your talent with your passion to discover your sweet spot in life. Now *that's* success!"

—**Jerry B. Jenkins**, novelist and biographer; founder, The Jerry Jenkins Writers Guild

"Growing up with a dad like Pat Williams means that from a very young age, I saw what passion looked like. As a child, I never understood why he was so excited to go to work every day, but now I know that it's because he was *passionate* about his message and he absolutely *loved* what he did. He always used to say, 'You can't fake passion. You either have it or you don't.' He sure had it, and still does—and it spreads like wildfire to everyone he meets. This book will help you pinpoint your 'sweet spot' and ignite a fire so bright, the world will sit up and take notice!"

—**Karyn Williams**, Christian recording artist

"Talent and passion. That's the ticket for success in any field. Pat Williams captures this concept beautifully in his latest book, *The Success Intersection*. Get ready for an impactful reading experience."

—**Steve Prohm**, head basketball coach, Iowa State University

THE SUCCESS INTERSECTION

THE SUCCESS INTERSECTION

WHAT HAPPENS When Your
TALENT Meets Your **PASSION**

Pat Williams
with Jim Denney

EBD
EMBASSY BOOKS
www.embassybooks.in

Published by :

Embassy Book Distributors
120, Great Western Building,
Maharashtra Chamber of Commerce Lane,
Fort, Mumbai - 400 023.
Tel : (91-22) 22819546 / 22818567.
Email : info@embassybooks.in
Website : www.embassybooks.in

ISBN: 978-93-86450-07-4

Printed and Bound in India by Repro India Ltd., India

This book is dedicated to

Gracyn Alyssandra Salazar,

our youngest grandchild,
in the hope that she will learn early in
life the principles in this book.

Contents

Acknowledgments 11
Foreword by Clint Hurdle 13
Introduction: *Telling My Secret* 15

1. Standing at the Intersection 19
2. Identify Your Talent 37
3. Identify Your Passion 61
4. Focus Your Talent 83
5. Focus Your Passion 105
6. Energized with Confidence 129
7. Multiply Your Success: *The Power of Teamwork* 153
8. Guiding Others to Their Success Intersection 171

Notes 195

Acknowledgments

WITH DEEP APPRECIATION I acknowledge the support and guidance of the following people who helped make this book possible:

Special thanks to Alex Martins, Dan DeVos, and Rich DeVos of the Orlando Magic.

Hats off to my associate Andrew Herdliska; my proofreader, Ken Hussar; and my ace typist, Fran Thomas.

Thanks also to my writing partner, Jim Denney, for his superb contributions in shaping this manuscript.

Hearty thanks also go to Andrea Doering and the entire Baker Publishing Group team for their vision and insight, and for believing that we had something important to say in these pages.

And finally, special thanks and appreciation go to my wife, Ruth, and to my wonderful and supportive family. They are truly the backbone of my life.

Foreword

Visit my offices at PNC Park in Pittsburgh or Pirate City in Florida, and the first thing you'll notice is my books. I have books lining my shelves and piled on my desk and stacked on the floor by the wall.

People often ask me, "Do you actually read all those books?" And yes, I actually do.

They're mostly books about leadership or teamwork or success or motivation. I read a lot of biographies about great sports heroes and great coaches like John Wooden and Vince Lombardi. And many of my favorite books have Pat Williams's name on the cover. The man knows how to inspire and motivate. He's a great leadership teacher. He understands success, because he's been living it throughout his career as a sports executive and cofounder of the Orlando Magic.

Full disclosure: Pat Williams is a longtime friend. But I'm not praising his books out of friendship. I'm saying all this because it's true. If you want to know what it takes to be successful in life, if you want to be inspired and fired up to achieve your goals, you've got to read Pat's books—and I strongly suggest you start with this one.

The Success Intersection will light a fire under you—and it will show you how to harness that fire to ignite your passion for success. This is the book I wish I had read at the beginning of my baseball career. And this is the book that will open your eyes and change your life, no matter where you are in your career.

From my years of experience as a player and a manager, I can tell you that everything Pat says in this book is the absolute truth. You may be loaded with talent, and you may think your talent alone will carry you to your goals. Wrong! Talent—even incredible talent—is simply not enough.

In addition to your great talent, you must have an intense passion for your goals. In this book, Pat will show you how to find and develop your greatest talent, and how to ignite your deepest passion so that you can achieve your dreams of greatness.

On the clubhouse wall of our spring training facility, there's a poster that reads, "We do not have time for just another day." In *The Success Intersection*, Pat will show you how to make every day special, meaningful, and passionate, so that you'll never live "just another day" for the rest of your life. He'll show you how to suck the marrow out of each moment, so that you'll not only *achieve* your dreams—you'll *live* your dreams.

But I don't want to steal Pat's thunder. You need to hear it straight from him.

So dig in, read this book. Highlight it. Take notes. Apply it. Live it.

Make a difference today.

Clint Hurdle,
Manager of the Pittsburgh Pirates
January 5, 2017

Introduction

TELLING MY SECRET

> We all have a unique gift or ability, like our very own superpower, which lives at the intersection of our talents and passions.
>
> **DAVID HASSELL**, entrepreneur and adventurer

ONCE, OVER DINNER with legendary UCLA basketball coach John Wooden, I said, "Coach, if you could pinpoint just one secret of success in life, what would it be?"

He thought for a moment, and then he said, "The closest I can come to one secret of success is this: 'A lot of little things done well.'"

In the spring of 2014, during a chat with my editor, she said, "So you asked Coach Wooden that question about one secret of success, and he said, 'A lot of little things done well.' Pat, what if someone asked *you* that question? Could you pinpoint one secret of success?"

I didn't even have to think about it. There's a simple formula for success that I have followed throughout my career. I said, "When your greatest talent intersects with your strongest passion, you've discovered your sweet spot in life."

My great consuming passion has always been sports, especially baseball. I was not merely a baseball fan, I was a baseball *megalomaniac*. I played baseball whenever I had the chance, from the time I was seven years old all the way through college at Wake Forest University, and finally in the minor leagues in Miami, Florida.

But while baseball was my greatest passion, it was not my greatest talent. I was good, but not great. After two years in the minor leagues, it was clear that my career as a professional baseball player had reached a dead end—but my career in professional sports was just beginning.

I found that my greatest talent lies in the realm of leadership, salesmanship, and promotion. In other words, I had great front office talent to match my passion for professional sports.

As a result, I've had an exciting career in sports—not as a player, as I had envisioned myself in my boyhood dreams, but as a sports executive, first in minor league baseball and later in the NBA. I've had the privilege of helping to assemble an NBA championship team (the 1982–83 Philadelphia 76ers) and helping to found an NBA expansion franchise (the Orlando Magic). I've spent more than fifty years applying my greatest talent to my greatest passion in life—and my life has been more fun than a theme park thrill ride.

Over the years, I've met successful people in every walk of life. In almost every highly successful man or woman I've met, I've recognized a quality I've found in myself: these highly successful individuals have learned to apply their greatest talent to the pursuit of their strongest passion in life. They are doing not only what they do well, but what they love most. *That* is why they are successful.

If you have great passion but no talent, you're going to fall flat on your face. If you are loaded with talent but doing a job you hate, every day of your life will be drudgery. But if your passion and your talent are focused intensely on a single goal, *you can't miss*. That's my secret of success—finding, and staying at, the intersection of talent and passion.

In the following pages, I'll share inspiring stories and practical insights that will show you how to recognize and maximize your talent, how to focus your passion and enthusiasm, and how to leverage your talent and your passion into a lifetime of amazing success. Let me help you find your sweet spot in life. Let's find your greatest talent, let's bring forth your strongest passion, and together we'll transform your life.

Turn the page with me. Let's get started.

1

Standing at the Intersection

> The greatest danger for most of us is not that our aim is too high and we miss it, but that it is too low and we reach it.
>
> Attributed to sculptor and painter **MICHELANGELO**

I CAN TELL YOU the exact moment my passion hit me.

The date was June 15, 1947, and I was seven years old. That was the day the course of my life was forever set, and nothing would ever deter me from that course.

On that day, my father took my sister Carol and me to Shibe Park in Philadelphia for a doubleheader, the Cleveland Indians versus the Philadelphia Athletics. Up to that time, I had only heard baseball games on the radio. I had never seen one with my own eyes, and I had no idea what to expect.

The moment I entered that historic ballpark, my senses were overloaded by the intense green of the grass, the fresh green paint on the ballpark walls, the brilliant white chalk lines on the field, and the crystal-clear blue sky overhead. I remember my father explaining the game to me, pointing out the scoreboard and the on-deck circle, pointing out the different players on the field and in the dugout. I was drawn into the suspense of the pitchers dueling with batters—and the intense action of a big hit and the poetic beauty of a double play.

To this day, I remember those sights and sounds, and my first taste of ballpark hot dogs and Cracker Jack. I remember cheering until I was hoarse. And that night, when I went to bed, I knew exactly what I wanted to be when I grew up—a ballplayer, a major leaguer.

That was my dream. That was my passion.

I pursued that passion all the way through elementary school and high school and into my college years at Wake Forest University. After four years catching on the Wake Forest team, I signed with the Philadelphia Phillies organization. In fact, I signed my contract in the office of Gene Martin, the Phillies farm director, and his office was located at Shibe Park—the very ballpark where my passion for baseball was born.

The Phillies organization gave me a $500 signing bonus on the spot. I had never seen so much money in my life. I knew I had the passion. I believed I had the talent. I was on my way to a big league sports career. First stop: the Phillies farm club in the Florida State League, the Miami Marlins.

What happened next? I'll return to that in a moment.

The point is that, throughout my life, my boyhood passion for sports has served and continues to serve me well.

My talent and my greatest passion intersected on the field of athletic competition—and I have had an exciting, rewarding career in the sports world for nearly fifty years.

Your Sweet Spot in Life

You are a unique and irreplaceable blend of interests, experiences, abilities, passions, and talents. There is nobody else in the world like you. Every day when you get up in the morning, you have to decide how to put your passions, your talents, and your time to the highest possible use. My goal for you is that as you read this book, you'll ask yourself, "What do I care about?" "What am I truly passionate about?" "What do I do well?" "What is my greatest area of talent?" The answers will energize you and organize your days so that you can reach your highest goals.

If you follow your passion and focus your talent, you are going to have a special "something" that defines you, that sets you head and shoulders above the crowd. You'll become noticed as someone who makes a rare contribution to the world, a person who makes a difference. You'll have something to offer that no one else has. You'll achieve a level of distinction that few other people ever know. As my late friend Zig Ziglar once said, "You are the only person on earth who can use your ability."

Robert Tuchman graduated from Boston University in 1993. His goal was to become a sports journalist. He had a degree from one of the top sports journalism schools in the country. Upon graduation, he made all the right moves in pursuit of his dream. He recorded a demo tape and assembled a résumé with references and testimonials from his internships.

He sent his package to hundreds of TV stations—and got no response.

So Tuchman took a position in the stockbroker trainee program at Lehman Brothers, the New York City investment banking firm. Tuchman's managers promised him and his fellow trainees that if they passed the brokerage exam, they would be offered full-time jobs as brokers with their own clients. Time passed, and Tuchman later recalled, "I quickly realized that, regardless of what I had been promised, management had no intention of promoting any of the trainees up the ladder, no matter how good we were. . . .That's when I started to dream of moving on."[1]

Robert Tuchman knew he had the talent to be a successful broker at Lehman Brothers or any other firm. In fact, it angered him to know that he was more talented and capable than most of the people he worked under. Yet he knew he didn't have a passion for selling stocks. Every morning, he opened the sports pages and read about all the people making a living in the sports world—sports reporters, sports agents, sporting event promoters—and he wished he could earn a living following his passion. "I *could* be a stockbroker," he later recalled, "but I didn't *love* the idea of being a stockbroker."[2]

Finally, Tuchman came to a decision: he had to find a way to connect his career to his passion for professional sports. He didn't know how he was going to do that, but he was determined to make it happen. To motivate himself, he asked himself the question, "Why not me?" He was sure that the people who worked in the sports world were no smarter than he was, no more talented than he was, no more energetic than he was. If they could do it, why couldn't he?

Armed with that motivational insight, he made the life-changing decision to leave his job as a Wall Street broker and accept a job with a Chicago-based company called Sports Profiles. The company needed an advertising sales rep in New York, and he took the job without any base salary—100 percent commission. The job was an eye-opener, because Tuchman discovered that his clients were interested in something called "added value." They wanted tickets to sporting events, travel packages, and similar perks more than they actually wanted to buy advertising.

A light came on. Tuchman realized he had stumbled onto a business idea that no one else was doing. Instead of using perks to sell advertising, why not sell the perks themselves? He asked himself, "What if I could combine my passion for sports with my sales ability?"[3]

Robert Tuchman decided to combine his greatest passion with his greatest talent. The result was a company built around selling corporate sports travel packages. Robert Tuchman was twenty-five years old when he founded his company—Tuchman Sports Enterprises (TSE)—in his one-bedroom apartment. His office furnishings consisted of a phone and a fax machine. Two years later, TSE was included on the Inc. 500 list of fastest-growing privately held companies—and in 2006, Tuchman sold his company to Premiere Global Sports for a sum in the millions of dollars.

Tuchman founded his company after asking himself, "Why not me?" So my question for you is: *Why not you?* You may have loads of talent for the job you're now doing. You may have a good retirement waiting for you (if you can just hold on for another fifteen or twenty years).

But is there an idea or a dream that has long been your passion—only you didn't dare let go of your "sure thing"? Tuchman, in his book *Young Guns: The Fearless Entrepreneur's Guide to Chasing Your Dreams and Breaking Out on Your Own*, recalls that many people told him he was crazy to leave the security of Lehman Brothers to pursue his passion for a career involving sports. After all, Lehman Brothers was a stable and secure industry giant, founded in 1850. When Tuchman left the company, he had no way of knowing that, on September 15, 2008, Lehman Brothers would file for bankruptcy—the largest bankruptcy filing in US history, and one of the tipping points that led to the 2008 global financial meltdown.

Often, a career path that seems safe and secure is actually fraught with peril—and sometimes a seemingly crazy decision to strike out on your own and follow your passion can be the sanest, safest course imaginable. There are no guarantees in this world—not even when your company has been around since 1850.

Jim Collins is a Stanford-trained business consultant who has worked for organizations as diverse as CNN, Johns Hopkins School of Medicine, the Girl Scouts, and the Marine Corps. He's the author of a number of business bestsellers, including *Good to Great: Why Some Companies Make the Leap . . . and Others Don't* and *Built to Last: Successful Habits of Visionary Companies* (with Jerry I. Porras). When I was researching this book, I was surprised to discover that Jim Collins has an almost identical formula for success to the one I have followed all my life. On his website, I found a three-part formula for success similar to my own intersection of talent and passion:

What are you passionate about?

What are you genetically encoded for? (In other words, what is your natural talent?)

What can you get paid for?[4]

The first two questions determine whether or not you have what it takes to be successful—great passion and great talent. The third question is a practical one: Is there a market for your passion and your talent? This is an important consideration.

You may have a passion for carving bars of soap into miniature replicas of the works of Michelangelo—and you might even have a great talent for it. But if you can't find anyone to pay you handsomely for your soap masterpieces, all the talent and passion in the world won't make you successful. So Jim Collins's third question is an important consideration.

When I combined my passion for sports with my talent for management, marketing, and speaking, I never doubted that I could get paid to do it. I had known a number of people in the Philadelphia Phillies front office for years, and I had been mentored and taught by some of the best in the sports management business. I knew there was a good living to be made in the front office.

And when Robert Tuchman launched his business selling corporate sports travel packages, he had already been making money selling sports travel packages as "added value" inducements to get people to buy advertising. He knew there was a market for his business. He knew he could get paid to merge his greatest passion with his greatest talent.

So as you are asking yourself, "What is my greatest passion in life? And what talent do I have for pursuing that passion?" make sure you are thinking in terms of dollars—and sense. Make sure there's a market for your greatest passion, and that someone will pay you to leverage your greatest talent.

When you have found that perfect intersection of passion and talent, and you know that you can make a living doing what you love, you have truly found your sweet spot in life. You are poised to achieve great things—and to reap great rewards.

The Barber with a Passion for Books

Rueben Martinez was born poor, the son of immigrant parents, in the tiny mining town of Miami, Arizona. Almost all of the jobs in the town were related to copper mining. Rueben possessed a curious mind. He was hungry for learning and loved to read, yet he had two strikes against him: the town had no public library, and Rueben's parents disapproved of reading.

"My mom couldn't stand me reading," he recalls. "My dad disliked it." His teacher would lend him a book every Friday for him to read over the weekend. One Saturday afternoon, his mother caught him reading and she sent him out to clean the yard. So Rueben hid the book under his bed and went out to do his chores. Two hours later, he returned to his room—but the book was gone. He searched and finally found what was left of the book amid the ashes in the woodstove.

"It just broke my heart," he recalls, "but I started reading more because of it."[5]

Forced to read in secret, Rueben had several hiding places where he stashed books and sneaked away to indulge his passion for reading. Every morning, he woke up early, sneaked over to the neighbor's porch, and read the morning newspaper. Then he carefully refolded the paper so the neighbor wouldn't suspect. One morning, the neighbor caught Rueben—but to the boy's surprise, the neighbor was pleased that Rueben was so hungry for knowledge, and he encouraged Rueben to keep reading.

At age seventeen, Rueben left Arizona and moved to Southern California. He fell in love with the California climate, the Pacific Ocean, and the California culture. He took an assortment of jobs—machine operator, factory worker, grocery clerk—and one day an ad for a barber college captured his attention. Most of the jobs he'd had in the past were dirty jobs that got his clothes grimy. But barbers always wore clean white smocks.

After completing barber college, Rueben Martinez opened his own one-chair barbershop in downtown Santa Ana, California. It turned out that he had quite a talent for cutting hair. He also had an intense passion for reading. He decided to combine his talent with his passion—and he hoped to pass that passion on to his customers, especially the Mexican-American young people in his community.

He moved bookcases into his barbershop, and stocked them with volumes from his personal library, all in Spanish. His books included novels ranging from the Cervantes classic *Don Quixote* to *One Hundred Years of Solitude* by Gabriel García Márquez, plus Spanish translations of American books, and important works of Spanish-language nonfiction. He would lend the books out to his customers free of charge. In 1993, he began offering Spanish-language books for sale.

Rueben Martinez became a tireless advocate for reading. He urged parents to read to their children, and he encouraged young people to make reading a lifelong habit. Eventually, his bookshop outgrew the barbershop and became the focus of his business. He moved to a larger storefront space around the corner and devoted the new store completely to books (including books for children) and the display of local art. He called his new store Librería Martinez Books & Art Gallery—and even though Rueben no longer cut hair, he kept a symbolic barber chair in the store as a reminder of the establishment's humble beginnings.

In 2004, Rueben Martinez was honored with a MacArthur Fellowship—a $500,000 "genius grant" awarded by the John D. and Catherine T. MacArthur Foundation. The award cited Rueben for "fusing the roles of marketplace and community center to inspire appreciation of literature and preserve Latino literary heritage." He has also been named a Presidential Fellow by Chapman University, where he helps attract Latino students into the university's science and math programs.[6]

There is no shortage of talented people in the world today. But there are all too few people who have learned to leverage their talent with a fiery passion. Talent without passion is like a tool locked up in a toolshed. It's passion that produces action and puts the tool to good use. People with passion are relentless. If you try to keep them from their passion, they only become more determined. Obstacles don't stop them. Opposition spurs them on. They slice through criticism like a chain saw through cotton candy. They are unstoppable.

And you can be unstoppable, too.

Don't Be a Successful Failure

Author and speaker Ken Robinson tells the story of an editor who once worked with him on a book he was writing. "She was an excellent judge of style and added hugely to the quality of the book," Robinson recalled. He asked the editor how she had chosen her career. She said she had moved into the publishing world in her forties after years of being a concert pianist.

Why had she changed professions? The editor explained that she had performed a concert in London with a full orchestra and a distinguished conductor. After the concert, she and the conductor had dinner together. The conductor complimented the excellence of her performance—then made an observation: "But you didn't enjoy it, did you?"

It was a startling question, and it forced her to admit that she hadn't enjoyed giving the performance. In fact, she admitted, she *never* enjoyed performing at the piano. "Why do you perform if you don't enjoy it?" the conductor asked.

"Because I'm good at it," she replied.

In other words, she had great talent as a pianist—but she had no passion for performing. Even though she had an amazing ability and artistry for performing on the concert stage, she was not at the intersection of talent and passion.

She explained her background to the conductor—born into a musical family, taking piano lessons and demonstrating talent at an early age, then earning a doctorate in music, followed by a concert career. In all those years, she had never asked herself if she enjoyed what she was doing. She pursued her career as a concert pianist because she was good at it, yet she had no passion for it.

Then the conductor made a statement that changed her life: "Being good at something isn't a good enough reason to spend your life doing it."

Soon after coming to that startling realization, this woman walked away from the concert stage and turned instead to the realm of books. There she discovered that she had a great talent for recognizing value in raw unpublished manuscripts, along with a talent for shaping those manuscripts into audience-pleasing bestsellers. Once she had found her place in the publishing world, she pursued her career with a genuine passion.[7]

Her success and joy in life came when she finally discovered the intersection of her talent and her passion.

We all have multiple talents. We all have abilities that could take us far in any of a number of directions. But the fact that we have a great talent doesn't mean we must build a career or a life based on that talent. What a tragedy it would be to be trapped by one's talent in a life without passion.

You may have a great talent, a wonderful gift, and it came so easily you felt it would be a crime to waste it. So you have pursued that "great talent"—you've studied it, practiced it, applied it, used it—yet you have no love for it, no passion for it, and your "great talent" gives you no joy or satisfaction. You may have been living your life to meet the expectations of others. The people around you think you are a great success at what you do—but you don't feel successful, because you don't *love* what you do.

You have a knack, a skill, an ability—and you are often surprised at how easily and naturally things come to you in this area of your life. But you don't enjoy it. In fact, when you daydream, you dream of doing something completely different. You find yourself thinking, *If only I had pursued this other talent—my life might be so different today. If only I had followed my passion, I might be a very different person today, doing very different things.*

Talent is a natural capacity for doing certain things extremely well. Passion is a natural love, enthusiasm, and even *obsession* for certain kinds of pursuits. As long as you are pursuing your "great talent" without passion, without enthusiasm, without love, you're always going to feel like a failure, no matter how "successful" other people say you are. You're always going to feel you've missed out on the best in life, because you settled for only pursuing your "great talent."

Passion is irrepressible. It stays with us for life, even if we don't pursue it. If we pursue some "great talent" because we believe it would be a shame to waste that talent, what are we *truly* wasting? I can tell you this: your passion will nag at you forever, warning you that you are wasting precious time that could be spent pursuing it.

So here we stand at the intersection of talent and passion, and you need to confront the same questions the concert pianist confronted with her orchestra conductor. He made a statement to her that ultimately changed her life—so I will make the same statement to you: "Being good at something isn't a good enough reason to spend your life doing it."

Don't just follow your talent. Your talent might lead you into a career that is prestigious, financially rewarding, and the perfect match for your natural abilities. But if that talent is not welded to your passions, then even if your face is on the cover of *Forbes* or *Vogue*, you're going to feel you're in a dead-end job.

You'll be a celebrated "success" and you'll feel like a failure.

Your Personal Odyssey

G. Richard Shell is a professor at the Wharton Business School. In his book *Springboard: Launching Your Personal Search for Success*, Shell tells the story of how he attended Princeton on a full military scholarship, intending to become a naval officer upon graduation. It was only natural, since he came from a military family and was the son of a retired Marine Corps general. But midway through his time at Princeton, he became troubled over US involvement in the Vietnam War, which he considered unjust. He surrendered his scholarship, became a pacifist, and (as he put it) "severed the narrative thread of my life. . . . I no longer recognized who I was."[8]

After college, Shell went from one job to another—house painter, social worker, political fund-raiser—but nothing satisfied him. So he set off on an around-the-world odyssey in search of himself. His journey began in a monastery in northern Greece, took him to the Sea of Galilee where he read the Bible "on location," then landed him in Istanbul, where he boarded the famed Magic Bus, the "hippie express" that traveled overland to India. During a stop in Kabul, Afghanistan, he stepped off the bus in a pouring rain, felt dizzy, then passed out and fell face-down in the mud.

When he came to, he was diagnosed with hepatitis. While being treated for the disease at a missionary hospital, he looked within and realized that his travels had brought him no closer to his destination. In fact, he had nearly died from the virulent liver disease. He discovered what Marcel Proust meant when he wrote, "The voyage of discovery lies not in seeking new horizons, but in seeing with new eyes."

Richard Shell began to see with new eyes. He continued on to India, then he returned to the home of his parents and reconciled with them. He attended law school, and one day, in his classroom, he experienced a sense of excitement and exhilaration about the educational process. "An especially gifted professor had me riveted to my seat," he recalled. Under that professor's teaching, Shell experienced a realization: "I wanted to be the person in the front of that room. I wanted to create that kind of excitement and insight for others. I wanted to be a teacher."

Richard always had a talent for leading and inspiring. Now he'd discovered the passion to connect to and magnify his talent. So Richard Shell's odyssey ended when he was thirty-seven years old, and he began his teaching career at the Wharton School.[9] As he taught, he studied all the great thinkers who wrote about what it means to be happy, to have a sense of purpose, and to be successful—thinkers like Aristotle, Plato, Benjamin Franklin, and Dale Carnegie.

In 2005, Richard Shell began teaching a seminar called "The Literature of Success: Ethical and Historical Perspectives." It was a curriculum he wished he could have taken when he was in college. Here are some of his key insights from his "Literature of Success" seminar:

1. *You must ask yourself: "What is success?"* Different people have different definitions of success. Some of us have simply absorbed our notions of success from the culture around us, from our entertainment media, and from family and friends. We have never actually stopped to ask ourselves: "What does success mean to me? How do I define what it means to have a successful life? It's not enough to simply

accept a definition of success that others have chosen for me—I have to define what success means to *me*."

The truest definition of success is not to be found in some distant land or on a mountaintop or among the stars. The truest definition of success comes from within. If you haven't defined what success looks like—on your own terms, according to your own values—how will you know when you've achieved it?

2. *You must discover what you do better than most people.* In other words, you must identify your talent. Shell encountered this question for the first time in a job interview. The prospective employer asked him a question he had never considered before: "What do you do better than most people?" We need to take inventory of our skills and natural abilities, because our talents help to shape our definition of success.

3. *You must ask yourself The Lottery Question.* This is a thought experiment that Shell also calls The Lottery Exercise. Let's say you have won the lottery—a $100 million prize. You have taken all the prudent steps to care for your family and invest your money wisely, and you will never have to worry about money again. Then ask yourself: "What will I do with the rest of my life?"

If you had no financial restraints or responsibilities and could do anything you wanted with your life, what would you do? Clearly, you would do the thing that most excites you, intrigues you, satisfies you, and makes you happy. *You would follow your passion.* Your answer to The Lottery Question will almost certainly reveal your greatest passion in life.

So, before you go on to the next chapter, I hope you'll take a few moments to consider those three questions: How do you personally define success? What do you do better than most people? What would you do with your life if you won the lottery?

If you honestly face those three questions, you'll find yourself moving toward that special place where your talent and your passion intersect and where the meaning of success becomes a reality for you. Arriving at that intersection is far more exciting than winning the lottery. Believe me, I know that feeling. I've been living at that intersection all my adult life.

So let's go further, let's go deeper. Let me show you how you can live there, too.

2

Identify Your Talent

> High achievers, we imagine, were wired for greatness from birth. But then you have to wonder why, over time, natural talent seems to ignite in some people and dim in others.
>
> **NANCY GIBBS**, author and presidential historian

MOST OF US THINK we know what our talents are. But identifying our talents isn't always as easy as we suppose. In fact, we may be completely unaware of some of our best and most life-changing talents. I speak from personal experience.

I previously talked about how my passion for sports was ignited when I saw my first baseball game at seven years old. The day I signed my contract to play pro ball for the Philadelphia Phillies farm club, the Miami Marlins, Phillies owner Bob Carpenter gave me a piece of advice with which to begin my sports career: "Keep your eyes and ears open—on the field and off."

So I drove from my home in Wilmington, Delaware, to Miami, Florida, where I reported to Andy Seminick, manager of the Miami Marlins. Andy had been a catcher with the Phillies in the late 1940s and early 1950s, and he was one of my boyhood idols. I was thrilled to have Andy as my first manager in the pros, and he made my time in Miami enjoyable and memorable.

The year was 1962, and we had quite a team, including a future Hall of Fame pitcher named Ferguson Jenkins. During my first season in Miami, I caught five of Fergie's seven victories. I hit .295 that season and went 18 for 61 with two doubles and a triple—a respectable showing. I wore uniform number 29, which had the name "S. Paige" sewn inside the collar; my uniform had once been worn by the great Satchel Paige himself.

What I didn't know at the time, and would only discover years later, was that there was a scouting report about me in a filing cabinet in the Phillies home office. That report had been filed by Phillies scout Wes Livengood when I was still a college player at Wake Forest. Wes had written, "Good receiver, adequate arm, poor speed, weak bat. His future is in the front office." I came back and played the 1963 season with the Marlins, but it was clear that my boyhood dream of becoming a major league baseball player was slipping away. I had the passion to match the dream, but my level of talent didn't match the intensity of my passion.

That was a painful realization to come to. Few losses hurt us more deeply than the loss of a dream. But even though I never made it to the major leagues, I'm grateful for the two years I had in minor league baseball.

My experience with the Miami Marlins in 1962 and 1963 laid the groundwork for the career I've had ever since. I can honestly say I know how it feels to ride the team bus on road trips, suffer the fears and insecurities of a professional athlete, and experience the highs and lows of competition. Many times over the years, I would sit down with a player and tell him he was being waived or traded—and I could honestly say I knew how he felt, how badly he wanted to succeed, and how much it hurt when the dream was crushed. Every leader needs a touch of empathy, and empathy comes from having walked a few miles in the shoes of your subordinate.

During my two seasons as a player, I followed Bob Carpenter's advice to keep my eyes and ears open. As I saw my playing career winding down, even before the season was over, I asked for a position in the front office. So general manager Bill Durney made me his assistant. I did everything from selling advertising and selling tickets to typing up news releases. Bill taught me the sports business from top to bottom. I still went to the field to catch batting practice and help warm up the pitchers, but I no longer suited up for games.

All my life, from age seven on, I had chased my dream. I had always known what I wanted in life. But at the end of the 1963 season, I faced an unknown future. My boyhood dream was shattered. What should I do with my life? Teach? Coach? Something else? I was starting life over from scratch.

At first, I didn't think I had any talent for sports management. I'd go out to sell ads for the Marlins game program, and come back empty-handed and dejected. "I'm a failure, Bill," I said. "I can't sell advertising to save my life."

Bill told me, "Your problem is that you think you're asking merchants to do you a favor and buy an ad. Pat, you need to change your thinking. You're doing the merchants a favor. For just a few dollars, you're putting their business in front of the buying public at every ball game. Advertising doesn't cost—it pays. Selling is the key to success in any business, and especially the baseball business. If you can sell, you'll always have a job in sports."

Then he taught me how to sell—and once I acquired the skill of selling, I was on my way. After serving my apprenticeship in Miami, the Phillies organization moved me to Spartanburg, South Carolina, where I became general manager of the Spartanburg Phillies. After a few seasons in Spartanburg, I moved to the NBA, where I eventually became general manager of the Chicago Bulls, then the Atlanta Hawks, and then the Philadelphia 76ers, where we won an NBA championship in 1983.

In 1986, I undertook the biggest challenge of my career—cofounding an NBA expansion franchise in central Florida, the Orlando Magic. In the process of building the Magic organization, I used every bit of passion I possessed, every bit of natural talent God had given me, and every skill I had learned in the sports management business, going back to those early days working alongside Bill Durney in Miami.

Throughout my early years, I had been focused on one thing: using my athletic ability as a professional baseball player. It had never occurred to me that I might have talents and abilities that would be perfectly suited to a career in sports management. As it turned out, I had gifts for identifying and hiring talented players, for management and organization, for marketing and promoting, and for public speaking. So my boyhood passion for sports is as strong as ever, even though my playing career ended after only two rather undistinguished years in minor league baseball.

My greatest passion and my greatest talents intersected in the field of sports management—but I would have missed out on this thrilling five-decade career if I had not identified a whole array of talents I had ignored in my early days.

As you have been reading my story, I hope you have been thinking about *your* story. I hope you've been asking yourself, "What talents do I possess that I don't even think of as 'talent'? What are some of my undeveloped skills that just might transform my life and send me soaring to success? What are my 'hidden' talents—and how do I identify them?"

I'm glad you asked.

The Bear Bryant Talent Matrix

Paul "Bear" Bryant, the late, great head football coach of the University of Alabama Crimson Tide, once observed that there are four kinds of people: "Those who have ability [or talent] and know it, those who have it and don't know it, those who don't have it and know it, and those who don't have it but don't know it."[1] We can visualize these four kinds of people with a simple four-quadrant graph that I call the Bear Bryant Talent Matrix:

The Bear Bryant Talent Matrix

1. I have a talent and I know it.	2. I have a talent but I don't know it.
3. I don't have a talent and I know it.	4. I don't have a talent but I don't know it.

The good news is that you don't have to remain in quadrant 2, 3, or 4. You can move to quadrant 1. You can know your talent and you can combine your talent with your passion and begin sprinting toward your dreams and goals. The matrix is a simple tool to help you visualize where you are on your journey toward discovering and leveraging your greatest talent.

If you have a passion for playing a sport, teaching and mentoring, starting a business, performing music, writing books, or some other field of endeavor that requires talent, the worst place to be is that fourth category—those who don't have talent but don't know it. Is there any greater disappointment than finding that the goal you've been aiming for all your life is completely out of reach? That's where I was when I realized I didn't have the talent to play in the major leagues. There were other people who knew I didn't have a big league playing career in my future. Baseball scout Wes Livengood had forecast my career when I was still in college: "His future is in the front office."

Phillies owner Bob Carpenter had read Wes Livengood's report on me, and he knew I didn't have big league talent, yet he gave me a contract to play in the minors. Why? Well, Bob was a longtime friend of my father's, who had died just after I graduated from Wake Forest. So Bob gave me a contract as a personal favor. But more than that, I think Bob also wanted to give me some experience to prepare me for a front office career.

I had lived my entire life up to that point in Bear Bryant's fourth category—those who don't have the talent but don't know it. Whenever we reach a point where it seems our plans have failed and our dreams have died, it's important to ask ourselves the question I asked at that point: "Is it possible I don't have the talent I think I do?" That question opens our minds to a whole range of possibilities we never considered before.

Once I discovered for myself that I wasn't going to play in the major leagues, I moved from the fourth category to the third category—those who don't have talent, and they know they don't have it. Knowing you don't have the talent to achieve your first-choice goals in life is not a happy place to be—yet reaching that nadir of disappointment can actually be the best thing that ever happened to you. That's the point where you say to yourself, "I don't have the talent I thought I did—now what?"

My dream was dashed—but I still had the rest of my life to live. My first career choice was gone, and I had never considered a second choice. What *new* goal could I set for my life? What talents did I have that I didn't know I had? These are the questions we must confront when we encounter a roadblock in life.

Thanks to the encouragement of Bill Durney, I soon moved from the third category to the second category—those who have talent but don't know it. Bill saw management talent in me that I hadn't even discovered yet. He told me I had a bright future in professional sports. It wasn't the future I had envisioned since boyhood, but in many ways, it was far better than my original dreams. After all, how many athletes get to enjoy a five-decade professional career in sports?

Bill Durney taught me everything he knew about sports management—and as I learned from him, I moved from the second category to the first: those who have talent and know it. Once I discovered my talent for sports management, I was on my way, and I never looked back. As a result, I've enjoyed an amazing and rewarding career.

I have been in all four squares of the Bear Bryant Talent Matrix. I started in square 4 and moved all the way up to square 1. Where do you fit in the matrix? Which of these four quadrants describes where you are today?

Now, there's a catch-22 in the matrix: what if you think you have the talent, but you don't? How do you find out what you don't know—especially if you don't know that you don't know it? How do you find out that you really don't have the talent to become, say, an actor or politician or major league baseball player?

You find out the same way I did: you pursue your dream with all the passion you have. You do everything you can to develop your skills and leverage your talent—and you see how far it takes you. As you pursue your dream, keep an open mind. Listen to your mentors, teachers, coaches, critics, and others who are objective and will give you the straight truth, even if it hurts.

Take a good hard look at your performance and your abilities. Don't lie to yourself. Honestly assess your talent level and be open to discovering latent talents you never knew you had.

I can't peer into your life and say, "Here's your hidden talent, here's what you need to do, here's the insight you've been missing." But I suspect there are people in your life who can tell you that and more. They can hold up a mirror to your life so you can see yourself and your many talents more clearly. No matter where you are on the Bear Bryant Talent Matrix, I hope you'll take time to reflect on your life, gather the wise insights of a few trusted friends, and start making plans and setting goals for the rest of your life.

Whatever you do, don't take one person's word for it. One teacher, coach, or critic could be wrong about you.

Award-winning author Harlan Ellison studied creative writing in college in the early 1950s. Ellison had been a student at Ohio State for a year and a half when he asked his writing professor, Dr. Shedd, for "an honest appraisal of my worth as a writer."

"Mr. Ellison," Dr. Shedd replied, "you cannot write. You have no talent. No talent whatsoever. No discernible or even suggestible talent. Not the faintest scintilla of talent. Forget it."

The brash young Ellison responded to his professor with a suggestion that is unprintable. That indecorous reply, combined with what Ellison described as "the lowest grade point average in the history of the University," resulted in his expulsion from Ohio State University.[2]

Upon leaving OSU, Ellison moved to New York City to pursue his dream of becoming a writer. There he met author and editor Lester del Rey (who later founded Del Rey Books, the fantasy and science fiction division of Ballantine Books). Del Rey mentored and encouraged the young Harlan Ellison. Within a few months after moving to New York, Ellison sold his first short story to a magazine for forty dollars.

During his first two years in residence in New York, Ellison sold more than a hundred stories and articles—and he sent copies of his published work to his old professor at Ohio State, Dr. Shedd. Ellison later moved to Los Angeles, where he wrote TV scripts for *Burke's Law*, *The Outer Limits*, *The Man from U.N.C.L.E.*, and *Star Trek*. His short story "The Man Who Rowed Christopher Columbus Ashore" was selected for the 1993 edition of *Best American Short Stories*.

All in all, not a bad showing for a writer with "no discernible or even suggestible talent." So don't let one lone critic persuade you that you have no talent. If, however, you are starting to hear a *chorus* of voices saying you lack sufficient talent in a certain field, perhaps it's time to stop, take a look at your skills and abilities, your track record and performance level, and ask yourself: "Do I really have what it takes to achieve these goals? Or are my natural talents and abilities suited to a *different* goal?"

These are questions you must ask yourself—and they are questions that *only* you can answer.

Steps to Identifying Your Talent

My son Thomas earned a dual master's degree at Seton Hall, New Jersey, in sports marketing and business administration. He was passionate about a career in the business side of professional sports. As part of his graduate program, he had to do an internship, so I offered to contact some sports executives in the Northeast on his behalf.

Randy Levine, president of the New York Yankees, called and told me that the team owner, George Steinbrenner, personally hired all interns, and all the internships for the coming season were taken. Mr. Steinbrenner and I went way back to 1972, when I was general manager of the Chicago Bulls and he was a minority owner. He became principal owner of the Yankees soon after he and I became acquainted. I was sorry to hear that the door was closed at the Yankees, but I knew that George would have helped if he could have.

The next day, however, Levine called back and said, "Because of your long association with Mr. Steinbrenner, he is willing to create a special internship for your son. Have him come to Yankee Stadium tomorrow, and we would like to meet with him."

An awestruck Thomas Williams arrived at Yankee Stadium for a meeting with the top brass, and they offered him a paid internship in the finance department. Thomas had an enjoyable first year with the Yankees. He impressed his employers with his talent and work ethic, and he hoped the organization would offer him a full-time job. Instead, they offered him a second year as an intern.

Thomas called me and expressed his disappointment. "Another year as an intern?" he said. "They say they like my work. Why don't they hire me?"

"Thomas," I said, "just do it. You're still learning and discovering your talent. Just keep working hard and doing everything they tell you, and I guarantee it will pay off."

He agreed to intern for another year, but at the end of that season, the Yankees still wouldn't offer him a permanent position. Around that same time, he heard that the Boston Red Sox had an internship available. So Thomas called up his ol' dad and asked, "What should I do? I really don't want to spend another year as an intern."

"Thomas," I said, "just go for it. This is your chance to show the Red Sox what you can do. Win the internship, and I guarantee you'll be glad you did."

So Thomas interviewed—and the Red Sox selected him. Thomas worked hard and demonstrated his talent. At the end of the season, the Red Sox offered him a job.

As it turned out, his first season as a full-time employee of the Boston Red Sox was 2004. And what happened in 2004? The Red Sox won the World Series for the first time since 1918. And because Thomas was a full-time employee of the Red Sox that year, he got a World Series ring valued at about $25,000.

Afterward I told him, "Thomas, most people working in baseball will spend decades in their career and never get within a thousand miles of a World Series ring. In your first season, you have a ring. An internship is all about revealing to you and your employers the talent and the passion you bring to the job. Aren't you glad you said yes to those internships?"

And Thomas agreed that he was very glad. He went on to spend a few more years with the Red Sox, then he moved on. He has built a very successful career for himself.

Success happens when we take the time to discover our talent and pursue that talent with a passion. Ambition is good, but temper your ambition with patience. Take the time you need to discover your talent and to prove your talent to the world. There just might be a championship ring in your future. Here are some additional ways you can discover your talents and reveal them to others so that you can advance toward your life goals:

1. *Ask yourself: "Where have I succeeded in the past?"* Consider all of the areas in your life where you have done well,

where you have accomplished something, where you have felt good about yourself, where you have been commended by teachers, coaches, and employers. What were the subjects in school that you enjoyed and excelled in? What subjects came easily for you and ignited your passion for learning? The ability to learn a task quickly and perform it with comparatively little effort indicates that your mind and body are "wired" for that task—meaning you have a talent for it.

What kinds of tasks and chores give you pleasure and enjoyment? What kinds of tasks do you enjoy doing over and over again? What tasks do you miss when you can't do them? What kinds of skills and talents do you see in other people that fascinate you and inspire you to emulate them? What kinds of talents and abilities do your heroes possess? Ask yourself these questions. The answers are indicators of your area of talent.

Make a list of all of these areas and subjects in which you have succeeded in the past. They point to where you would likely succeed in the future—and they indicate where your true talents lie. You may find that you have never before considered a career in some of these areas. But once you have written them down, they become possibilities in your mind.

So explore those possibilities.

2. *Ask people to tell you what talents they see in you.* Select a few people you can count on to level with you for your own good—close friends, perceptive family members, mentors, teachers, coaches, and employers. Ask, "What talents do you see in me? If I were to change careers, what career do you think I might excel in?" Listen with an open mind and write

down their answers for future reference. Note especially when you get the same or similar answers from several people.

If you know someone who has a track record for recognizing talent, all the better. Go to that person and ask him or her to give you an honest assessment of your talents and abilities.

A number of years ago, I interviewed Disney animation artist X Atencio, who helped animate such classic films as *Pinocchio* and *Dumbo*. Atencio, who was born Francis Xavier Atencio, told me he had spent nearly thirty years in feature animation, and he expected to continue animating until he retired. But one day in 1967, Walt Disney came to him and said, "X, it's time for you to move." And Walt sent him to the Disney division in charge of building attractions for Disneyland. "I didn't know anything about building attractions," he told me. "I was an animator."

When he arrived at his new office, he said, "Walt sent me. What do you want me to do?" But Walt hadn't told anyone he was sending X over to work on attractions, so no one had an assignment for him to do. X waited and waited, and finally Walt called him and said, "X, I want you to write the script for the new Pirates of the Caribbean attraction. We'll have pirates and townspeople, and I want you to write all their dialogue." X said, "Are you sure you've got the right guy? I've never written a script before." Walt said, "I know you can do this."

So X became a writer. He began by scripting dialogue for drunken pirates who were selling brides at an auction. He showed it to Walt, who said, "Keep going, X, this is good."

Later, X came back to Walt and said, "I think the attraction needs a song that plays throughout. I've come up with a melody line and some lyrics, just to show you what I have in mind. But you should really put your songwriters in charge of the music." Walt said, "Oh no, you're doing just fine. Show this to George Bruns, our music director, and he will score it."

And the song X wrote—a song written by an animator who had never written a song in his life—became world famous: "Yo Ho, Yo Ho, a Pirate's Life for Me." And X went on to write another classic Disneyland theme, "Grim Grinning Ghosts," for Disneyland's Haunted Mansion.

X Atencio had a passion for animation, for telling a story. He didn't know that he was a scriptwriter or a songwriter until Walt Disney gave him the job. Walt identified talents that X didn't even know he had, and Walt gave X the chance to discover those talents and put them to good use in combination with his passion.

Is there a "Walt" in your life who can identify undiscovered talents within you? What have others asked you to do that seemed out of your area of expertise? Next time, instead of saying, "I can't do that; I've never done that before," consider saying, "Sure, I'll try anything. Who knows? I may have talents I've never even used before."

3. *Take a personality inventory test.* Examples include the International Personality Item Pool (available at www.personal.psu.edu/~j5j/IPIP/), the Myers-Briggs Type Indicator (available at CPP, www.cpp.com/services/professionalservices.aspx), and the MAPP career assessment test (available at www.assessment.com/). These personality tests can help you to understand whether you are an introvert or an extrovert, how you learn new information and apply what you know, whether you operate more on thinking or on feeling, whether

you are more organized or more spontaneous, whether you are more cooperative or more competitive, and so forth. Armed with these insights and an increased self-awareness, you'll be able to better understand the talents you possess—and the best ways to use your unique array of talents.

4. *Be willing to try new things.* The only way to discover talents you never knew you had is by doing things you've never done before. Take a class in painting, and you might discover you have a latent gift as an artist. Volunteer at a homeless shelter or afterschool tutoring program, and you might just discover interests, talents, and a brand-new passion for helping others. Join Toastmasters, and you might gain a new career as a public speaker. (By the way, I was scared to death of public speaking when I was in high school, overcame my fear in college, and I now earn a significant portion of my living as a professional speaker.)

Oh, and have you ever considered performing in the ballet?

Steve McLendon, a 320-pound nose tackle for the New York Jets (formerly with the Pittsburgh Steelers), has been taking ballet classes since his college years. "I needed like an extra credit or two," he recalls, "and the first day when I walked into class, there were nothing but females in there. Then [the teacher] told me it could help me with football."[3] McLendon believes ballet dancing helps to strengthen his lower body, especially his ankles and feet, and helps him to prevent injury.

But ballet is more than a strength and conditioning program for Steve McLendon. He actually enjoys the dance, the music, and the discipline. His longtime ballet teacher, Stephanie Kibler, says that he works hard at mastering the artistry of ballet—and he clearly enjoys it. "I work him harder than the majority of women will ever work in a ballet setting," she explains. "He does it well. He might have sweat dripping off him and looking at me like I'm crazy, but he does it. . . . He's mastering the craft of ballet. He's not in there just for football."[4]

McLendon has also convinced fellow defensive linemen Ziggy Hood and Al Woods to join him at ballet class. After attending a class with McLendon, Al Woods said, "You think of ballet, you think of tutus and ladies jumping around and things of that nature, but after I actually did the class, I felt like I had played a whole football game."[5]

So be open to new experiences. Always be ready to stretch yourself in new directions. Keep your eyes and mind open to new possibilities—and you might discover life-changing talents you never knew you had.

5. *Pay attention to any talent or ability that you discover.* We often forget how truly unique we are as human beings. There are many people who write books—but no one else brings quite the same combination of experiences and passions to a book that I do. There are many people who give speeches—but no one else brings quite the same message and style that I do. There are many people who work in the field of sports management—but no one else has the exact blend of experiences, insights, and abilities that I bring. This doesn't mean I feel superior to anyone else in any of these fields—it just means that I am uniquely myself, and no one else is me.

You are uniquely you. Your talents and abilities make you who you are. And your uniqueness might well be the key to finding your most important talent. Ask yourself, "What do I do, think, or say that seems obvious to me, but others remark on?" Often our talent comes so naturally to us we can't imagine it's not that way for others—we don't see it as a talent at all.

Catherine Gray is the director of training at The White House Project, a nonprofit organization that seeks to increase the representation of women in American institutions, businesses, and the government. She is also a leader, motivational speaker, entrepreneur, and filmmaker.

When she was nine years old, Catherine and her classmates were in a coeducational gym class. All the students, boys and girls, were to throw a softball as far as they could, and the distance of their throws would be measured. The class was divided with all the boys in one line on one side of the field, all the girls in a line on the other side. There were two tape measures laid out on the field, a shorter tape measure for the girls and a longer tape measure for the boys.

When it was Catherine's turn to throw, she hurled the ball with all her might. It landed several feet beyond the end of the tape measure. So the teacher had her throw the ball a second time. Again, it landed well beyond the end of the tape measure. So the teacher led Catherine and the other girls over to the boys' line, and all the students, boys and girls, threw from the same line and were measured against the same tape measure.

Catherine Gray's story is a metaphor that illustrates what happens when we discover our talent and put it to good use. Until she threw that ball, she didn't know she had that level of talent. Once she demonstrated her talent, she was able to place herself and the other girls on an equal basis with the boys. By unleashing her talent, she broke the barrier that separated the boys from the girls—and she has been breaking down gender-based barriers ever since.[6]

We all have talent, and we all have a part to play. When you and I discover our talents and put them to good use, we too can break down barriers and help ourselves and others become all we are meant to be. Whether you have a talent for throwing a softball, playing the violin, writing a novel, or peering into a microscope, make sure you play your part. Be uniquely who you are. Discover your talents and use them to the fullest. By doing so, you will help bring beauty, harmony, and justice to the world.

6. *Always work hard and do your best.* In 1934, a twenty-two-year-old writer named Arnold Samuelson graduated from journalism school at the University of Minnesota. The first thing he did after graduation was to hitchhike from Minnesota to Key West. His goal was to meet novelist Ernest Hemingway and learn all he could about writing fiction. He fully expected Hemingway to tell him to get lost—but Samuelson figured he had to try. Arriving in Key West, Samuelson located Hemingway and introduced himself.

Hemingway later said that he felt "both flattered and appalled" that this young man had hitchhiked all the way from Minnesota just to ask "a few questions about writing." So Hemingway—who had just bought a thirty-eight-foot fishing boat named *Pilar*—offered Samuelson a job as a deckhand for a dollar a day. Samuelson jumped at the chance to become the apprentice of Ernest Hemingway. On one occasion, Samuelson asked Hemingway what it takes to be a great writer.

"Seriousness is one thing you've got to have," Hemingway replied. "Big-time writing is the most serious business there is, and imaginative writing is the peak of the art. Another thing you've got to have is talent."

Samuelson asked, "How can a man know if he's got talent?"

"You can't. Sometimes you can go on writing for years before it shows. If a man's got it in him, it will come out sometime."[7]

Samuelson would write stories and story fragments, then show them to Hemingway, who would offer his critique and advice. It became very much a mentor-apprentice relationship.

One day Samuelson asked Hemingway, "Do you think I'll ever make it as a writer?"

"You are getting better. Much better. If you have talent, it will show up later. . . . Just keep working."[8]

Arnold Samuelson spent the better part of the year working for Hemingway, questioning him, and learning from him. He carefully recorded a narrative of his adventures and conversations with Ernest Hemingway. But in spite of Hemingway's encouragement, Samuelson never went on to a career in writing. The manuscript about his year with Hemingway lay undiscovered until years after his death. It was published by Random House in 1984 under the title *With Hemingway: A Year in Key West and Cuba.*

It's a mystery why Arnold Samuelson never became a professional writer. He certainly seemed to have a passion for writing. After all, it takes a lot of passion to hitchhike from Minnesota to Key West in the hope of meeting a literary hero. Perhaps Samuelson lacked talent as a writer—though the quality of the writing in *With Hemingway* would seem to indicate that he did in fact have talent. For whatever reason, Samuelson's only literary achievement was that one book, published years after his death.

But here's the point of the story—the moral, if you will: *it takes hard work to discover your talent*. Hemingway gave Samuelson some very good advice: "If you have talent, it will show up later. . . . *Just keep working*." Very few people discover their talent while snoring in a hammock. The harder you work and the more you demand of yourself, the more talent and ability you will discover. Hard work reveals talent.

As supreme commander of the allied forces in Europe, General Dwight D. Eisenhower ordered the D-Day invasion that proved to be the turning point of World War II. Eisenhower went on to become the thirty-fourth president of the United States from 1953 until 1961. But the world might never have heard of Eisenhower had he not worked hard and pursued excellence while rewriting a couple of book chapters that were never published.

During the late 1920s, Eisenhower worked for the American Battle Monuments Commission under the direction of General John J. Pershing. Eisenhower found it to be a job that didn't challenge him, didn't excite him, and didn't utilize his talent and ability—yet he respected General Pershing and he did his work to the best of his ability. In 1929, Eisenhower was transferred to the War Department, where he worked as an executive assistant to Brigadier General George Moseley. In November of that year, Eisenhower's old boss, General Pershing, contacted him and asked for help in writing his memoirs about World War I. He especially wanted Eisenhower to review the chapters on the battles at Saint-Mihiel and the Argonne.

So Eisenhower read the chapters and returned them to General Pershing with a suggestion that he rewrite them in a narrative style instead of a somewhat confusing diary format. Pershing then asked Eisenhower to rewrite the chapters in the narrative style and send the revised chapters to Colonel George C. Marshall for review. So Eisenhower rewrote the chapters and sent them to Colonel Marshall, who discussed Eisenhower's work with Pershing.

After meeting with Pershing, Marshall visited Eisenhower's office and the two men met for the first time. Eisenhower later recalled their conversation. Marshall, he said, "remarked that he read over my chapters. 'I think they're interesting. Nevertheless, I've advised General Pershing to stick with his original idea. I think to break up the format right at the end of the war would be a mistake.' He remarked, rather kindly, that my idea was a good one. Nevertheless, he thought that General Pershing would be happier if he stayed with the original scheme."

Eisenhower and Marshall would not meet again for more than a decade—but what Eisenhower didn't know at the time was that George Marshall had (as historian Michael E. Haskew observed) "a keen eye for talent" and he kept a little black book in which he recorded the names of junior officers that showed extraordinary potential. Eisenhower's excellent work in rewriting those two chapters—even though his work was never published—made a great impression on George Marshall. Years later, when General Marshall became army chief of staff under Franklin D. Roosevelt, he elevated many of the officers listed in that little black book, including such illustrious commanders as Joseph Stillwell, Omar Bradley, George S. Patton Jr., Walter Bedell Smith, and yes, Dwight D. Eisenhower.[9]

So always work hard and always do your best. Your talents, which might not seem like they are being put to good use this very moment, could significantly impact your life in years to come.

7. *Hone the talents you know you have.* By practicing the abilities you are aware of, you often discover other talents you didn't know you had. You and I are capable of more than we know, more than we can imagine. We have talents—genetic advantages in certain tasks—that we don't realize. And we have the ability to learn and acquire skills in areas where we don't have a natural talent.

By using all of the natural talents we possess, we learn and grow, we acquire new experiences, we take on new challenges, we increase our confidence, and we discover we can do far more than we ever thought possible. By continually practicing our talents, we build so-called "muscle memory," which enables us to turn a task we have to think about into an automatic response.

If you are an athlete, practicing your athletic talents may reveal to you hidden talents for teaching and coaching, interacting with young people, public speaking, organizational leadership and management, and more. If you are a writer, practicing your writing ability may reveal to you hidden talents for telling stories through filmmaking or acting. If you have a talent for creating wealth in the business world, you may discover related talents that can be put to good use in other fields—teaching young people how to save and invest, or providing fiscal leadership in a church or charitable organization.

If you consistently practice your known talents, other talents will emerge or be strengthened. And previously unimagined opportunities for success will present themselves.

The first step in finding your success intersection is to identify your talent—not just one talent, but the full array of your many talents. And that leads us naturally to the second step: finding your passion.

3

Identify Your Passion

> Success consists of going from failure to failure without loss of enthusiasm.
>
> **WINSTON CHURCHILL**, statesman

A FEW YEARS AGO, I gave a presentation and book signing at a large chain bookstore. Afterward, I thanked the bookstore staff, then I got in my car and started to pull away. I heard someone shout, "Mr. Williams! Mr. Williams!"

I stopped the car and rolled down the window. A young man ran up to me. "I couldn't get here in time for the book signing," he said. "I was afraid I'd missed you."

"Take a moment to catch your breath," I said. "How can I help you?"

"I just have one question: if you could name one quality a person needs to succeed, what would it be? What one quality stands head and shoulders above all the rest?"

"Actually, there are *two* qualities that are absolutely essential to success. First, you must have the *talent* to succeed in your chosen profession. If you're five-foot-two and your dream is to be a center in the NBA, you need to find a different dream.

"But once you know you've got the talent you need, the other essential quality you must have is *passion*. You've got to love what you do. What is your passion? What really gets you excited? Figure out how to start your own business around it or how to get someone to pay you to do it, then pursue your passion. If you can make a living following your passion, you'll have a head start on a successful life. As someone once said, 'Success is not the key to happiness. Happiness is the key to success. If you love what you do, you'll succeed.'"

Smiling broadly, he jotted some notes in a notebook, then thanked me and walked away. I think the world may be hearing more from that young man in years to come.

In the last chapter we talked about your talents. But talent is only half of the equation. Talent can only take you so far. Passion—loving what you do, believing in what you do, being fiercely and intensely committed to what you do—completes the equation and amplifies your talent, taking you to success.

When Philadelphia Phillies front office advisor Pat Gillick was general manager of the team, he told an interviewer, "Talent is overrated," adding that while talent is important, other qualities—such as mental toughness, character, and passion—are even more important. "These are the things," he said, "that cannot be measured."[1]

In 2012, Yahoo! Finance and *Parade Magazine* conducted a joint survey of 26,000 Americans to find out how people felt about their careers. At a time when unemployment was high and it seemed Americans should feel fortunate to even have a job, almost 60 percent of respondents said that they were dissatisfied in their jobs and wished they were in a different career. The survey showed that while people in entry-level "McJobs" were unhappy with their career choice, people making good money in white-collar jobs were also unhappy.[2]

Clearly, money is not the primary issue in career dissatisfaction. In fact, I suspect that the biggest factor for most people might well be a *lack of passion* for the work they do. If you are only working for a paycheck—even if it's a very fat paycheck—you are not going to be happy in your career. Success is not the key to career happiness. Happiness is a byproduct of passion for your career. If you are passionate about your work—whether you are president of the United States or a sanitation engineer—you are going to feel happy and successful in your job.

Does that statement surprise you? Is it possible to be a successful sanitation engineer? Yes, absolutely—if you have a passion for the job. I have met such people, and so has Dr. Art Lindsley of the Institute for Faith, Work & Economics. After conducting a study of the ways people find their calling in life, Dr. Lindsley wrote, "In the hundreds of vocational profiles I have done, I have found some interesting cases. . . . I interviewed one man whose greatest desire was to be a janitor of the local school and make its floors shine. Some love to star and others want to be out of the spotlight."[3]

As Dr. Martin Luther King Jr. once said, "If it falls your lot to be a street sweeper, sweep streets like Michelangelo painted pictures, like Shakespeare wrote poetry, like Beethoven composed music; sweep streets so well that all the host of Heaven and earth will pause and say, 'Here lived a great street sweeper, who swept his job well.'"[4]

Do you want to be successful in your life and in your chosen career? Then identify your passion and pursue it for all you're worth. Once you've found the goal that excites you, motivates you, and stirs your passion, you are well on your way to a rewarding and successful life. Even if you are utilizing all your talent, even if you are pursuing a career that seems tailor-made for your gifts and abilities, even if you are making great money and you enjoy all the outward trappings of success—if you don't have a passion for what you do, you might as well be an assembly line robot welding widgets onto gadgets. All your wealth will seem pointless, your so-called success will seem hollow, and your career will seem meaningless and mechanical.

Ohio surgeon Michael S. Kavic, MD, once wrote in a medical journal that when interviewing candidates for a surgical residency, the qualifications he looked for were not necessarily the qualities you might expect—a high intellect, excellent hand-eye coordination, an easygoing temperament, or even extensive medical knowledge. All of these qualities have to do with mere talent. Dr. Kavic said that the quality he looked for in a candidate, above all else, was *passion*.

"Because of a perceived passion for excellence, the public holds surgeons in high regard," he explained. "The privilege of performing a surgical intervention within the human body has attracted the best and brightest of our youth for generations. A surgeon, with rare exception, truly loves the practice of surgery. A surgeon will render operative care to the best of his ability, to the least of our society, day or night, regardless of the hours worked or patients seen."

A surgeon who works inside the human body, he added, should view a surgical career as being "swept away in the grand drama of working in God's temple." Passion—a "fire in the heart"—is what truly separates a merely talented scalpel technician from a genuine healer.[5]

What is true for great surgeons is also true for you and me: when your greatest talent intersects with your strongest passion, you have discovered your sweet spot in life. Without passion, talent has no focus, no direction. And without talent, passion has nothing to work with. You must have talent *and* passion, working together, synergizing each other, in order to achieve lasting success and a meaningful life.

Your First Responsibility

At this point, let's remind ourselves of our definition of *talent* and *passion*: Talent is a natural capacity for doing certain things extremely well. Passion is a natural love, enthusiasm, and even obsession for certain kinds of pursuits. Our passions grip us, motivate us, excite the imagination, and define who we are. At the deepest core of our being, *we are our passions*, because our passions are the things we care about most in life. Our passions drive us and announce to the world who we are and what we are all about.

As human beings, we all have many passions. From my boyhood, my one overriding passion was sports, especially baseball. As I matured, I acquired other passions, and some of those passions have become even more intense and compelling to me than my lifelong obsessions with sports. For example, I'm extremely passionate about my faith in God. As a father, I'm intensely passionate about family, about my children and grandchildren, and about the importance of adoption (as my fourteen adopted children from four different countries will attest). I'm passionate about leadership, mentoring, influencing the next generation, public speaking, and writing books. All of these are passions in my soul that drive me and rule my life and define who I am as a human being.

Over my years in the NBA, I have known many, many basketball players—athletes who are at the absolute pinnacle of their profession. I can tell you that, without exception, all of the truly great basketball players have been driven by an absolute passion for the game. They eat, sleep, and breathe basketball. They are possessed and obsessed with a love of the game. The mere sight of a basketball makes a player's hands itch to hold it, dribble it, shoot, and score. The thought of losing is anathema to a passionate player. Whenever a great player is away from the game, he practically goes into withdrawal.

That's why, if you are truly passionate about your goals in life, you can't help but achieve them. If you are passionate, you won't let anything stop you. You won't let anyone stand in your way. Your passion will drive you straight through any obstacle or opposition to your ultimate success.

This intense obsession we call passion enables us to focus our concentration and magnify our awareness. It enables us to react more swiftly and effectively to changing circumstances. Passion turns work into play and transforms a career into a thrill ride. Passion adds color and emotion and meaning to our everyday lives.

One of the first and most important challenges we face is that of *identifying our passion in life*. Until we have a passion that grips our minds and captures our imaginations, we are just sleepwalking through life. Until we have identified our passion, life has no direction, no focus, no goal.

Condoleezza Rice served as national security advisor in President George W. Bush's first term, and secretary of state in the second term. On May 12, 2012, the former secretary of state gave the commencement address at Southern Methodist University. She told her story, a story about finding and following her passion in life. She began by telling the students that their first duty in life is to "find and follow your passion. Now, I don't mean just any old thing that interests you, or your career. I mean something you really believe is a unique calling to you—in other words, something that you can't live without."

How did Condoleezza Rice find her passion? It wasn't easy. In fact, finding her passion involved a good deal of trial and error. She entered college as a music major, having studied music since she was three years old. She had talent and was passionate about becoming a concert pianist. But at the end of her sophomore year in college, she visited the Aspen Music Festival School in Colorado—and there she met twelve-year-olds who could flawlessly sight-read music it had taken her a year to learn. Her dream of performing at Carnegie Hall vanished in a puff of smoke.

So Condi Rice went home and informed her parents that she was changing her major. Her mom and dad asked, "What are you changing your major to?" She replied, "I don't know." "Don't you know what you want to do with your life?" "No, but it's my life." "But it's our money. Find a major."

She returned to college and desperately searched for a major to declare. In reality, she was searching for a new passion to replace her shattered dream of being a pianist. She tried English literature—and hated it. She tried government—and hated it even more.

In the spring quarter of her junior year, she walked into a class taught by an expert in Soviet affairs, Josef Korbel (whose daughter, Madeleine Albright, would one day become the first woman secretary of state, serving in the Clinton administration). "With that one class, I was hooked," Rice said. "I discovered that my passion was Russian." She was fascinated with Russian culture, Russian history, and the politics of Soviet Russia.

Years later, when Condoleezza Rice served in the George H. W. Bush administration, the president asked her to accompany Soviet Secretary-General Mikhail Gorbachev and his wife Raisa on their journey across America, from Washington to California. As she chatted with the Gorbachevs on the south lawn of the White House, accompanied only by the Secret Service, a thought occurred to her: *I'm really glad I changed my major*.

Condoleezza Rice's passion for all things Russian and a talent for diplomacy led her to a life in government, a field she had once thought she hated. And she never lost her passion for music. "Those first passions never leave you," she said. And in 2002, while she was serving as national security advisor, Condoleezza Rice had the privilege of performing on a national stage. Cellist Yo-Yo Ma called her and told her he would be receiving the National Medal of the Arts, and he asked her to accompany him on the piano. Without hesitation, she said yes.

So in April 2002, at Constitution Hall in Washington, DC, Condoleezza Rice performed a duet, accompanying one of the great cellists of our time. "I was not playing with Yo-Yo Ma because I was the world's greatest pianist," she said. "I was playing with Yo-Yo Ma because I was the National Security Advisor who could also play the piano. Avocations sometimes pan out as well. So your first responsibility is to find your passion."[6]

A Passion for the Game

On July 8, 1968, when I was a minor league baseball general manager in Spartanburg, South Carolina, I walked into my office and found a phone message on my desk. It was from Jack Ramsay and he was calling from Inglewood, California.

The only Jack Ramsay I had ever heard of was the general manager of the Philadelphia 76ers. Why would the GM of the NBA franchise in Philly be calling me? And why would he call from Inglewood, California? Certainly, it couldn't be *that* Jack Ramsay.

So I returned the call—and was amazed to discover that it was in fact *that* Jack Ramsay. He was in California to negotiate a trade between the 76ers and the Los Angeles Lakers.

"Pat," he said, "our head coach has resigned, and I've agreed to coach the team this season. That won't leave me any time to manage the team, so we need a business manager. Would you be interested in the job?"

"Yes, absolutely!"

"Fine. Let's get together in Philadelphia to talk about it."

So I flew to Philadelphia and Jack offered me a three-year contract. I would be in charge of promotion, publicity, ticket sales, and much more. It was essentially the general manager's job minus responsibility for players and personnel. To this day, I don't know where Jack heard about me or why he felt he could entrust the 76ers to a twenty-eight-year-old kid, fresh out of minor league baseball.

Jack plucked me out of the minor leagues and put me in the big leagues. I had always thought that my future would be in baseball—but Jack Ramsay gave me a new vision of a future in basketball. Suddenly, my life was a whole new ball game.

His nickname was "Dr. Jack," because he had earned a doctorate in education from the University of Pennsylvania. After coaching the 76ers, he went on to coach the Buffalo Braves, the Portland Trail Blazers, and the Indiana Pacers. In 1977, his first season with the Trailblazers, he coached the team to its first NBA title. After retiring from coaching, Dr. Jack spent the next quarter century as a broadcast sports analyst. After his death in 2014, Michael Mink of *Investors Business Daily* published a profile headlined "Jack Ramsay Had a Passion for Basketball That Won Out."

Excerpts from Jack Ramsay's 2011 book, *Dr. Jack on Winning Basketball*, illustrate his lifelong passion for basketball, for competing, and for winning. His passion for basketball took hold on the day his father hung a basket on the wall of the barn at his Connecticut home. "Every day during the school year," Jack wrote, "in all but the worst weather, I'd make a beeline for the barn the minute after I got home. That was my haven—and my heaven. I spent hours there shooting and dribbling, rebounding shots."

Dr. Jack's passion for competing intensified during World War II, when he volunteered for service in the Naval Combat

Demolition Unit, the elite forerunner of the Navy SEALs. He was training for the toughest, most dangerous assignment imaginable—leading a platoon in an invasion of mainland Japan. He was spared having to undertake such a dangerous mission when America's most formidable secret weapon, the atomic bomb, convinced the Japanese to surrender in August 1945.

"I never forgot the competitive lessons learned during my training with the [Naval Combat Demolition Unit]," Ramsay wrote. He applied those lessons throughout his coaching career. During that career he compiled an 864-783 record as an NBA head coach. In his twenty full NBA seasons, his teams missed the playoffs just four times. He was inducted into the Hall of Fame in 1992.

Looking back on his career near the end of his life, he reflected on his obsessive passion for the game: "In all of that time, the lure of the court never diminished for me. I still feel the same way about all of my associations with basketball, whether playing, coaching, conducting clinics, doing radio and television broadcasts of games or writing about it, [I still have] a deep, abiding love for the game."[7] Jack Ramsay became one of the great coaches of the game because of his passion for basketball.

But is it possible to be successful in an endeavor that you *don't* feel passionate about? The answer to that question may surprise you.

Passion from an Unexpected Source

Curtis Martin was one of the dominant running backs in the NFL throughout his eleven-year career with the New

England Patriots and the New York Jets. He retired with the fourth highest total rushing yards in NFL history, and was inducted into the Pro Football Hall of Fame in 2012. And here's the most surprising fact about Curtis Martin: *he didn't like football*. And he *especially* didn't want to play for the Jets.

But don't you need *passion* in order to be successful in any endeavor? Absolutely. Without question. The intersection of talent and passion is the key to success. But if Curtis Martin had no passion for football or for his team, why was he so successful?

Answer: Curtis Martin was driven and obsessed by a different passion—a passion that had little to do with the game of football. Listen to his story, and all will become clear.

As a boy, growing up in inner-city Pittsburgh, Curtis Martin didn't think he'd see his twenty-first birthday. His father was a violent, abusive man who used to torture his mother, beating her, punching her in the face, and burning her with cigarettes.

Curtis grew up in a dangerous neighborhood. When he was fifteen, a robber put a gun to his head and pulled the trigger. The gun didn't fire. The gunman pulled the trigger a total of seven times, yet the gun didn't fire. Finally, in frustration, the assailant pointed the gun away—and it fired. Curtis Martin felt his life had been spared by a miracle.

In high school, Martin played basketball in his sophomore year but didn't go out for sports in his junior year. His mother feared that too much free time would lure him into the violence of the streets, so she insisted he go out for football. Though he didn't like the sport, he played football his senior year. It turned out he was a naturally gifted athlete.

So Curtis Martin discovered the talent to succeed in football, but where was the passion? The only person who was obsessed with keeping Curtis Martin on the football field was his mother. In that one season of high school football, Curtis ran for 1,705 yards and scored twenty touchdowns. His outstanding performance attracted the attention of college football programs around the country, but Curtis accepted a football scholarship from the University of Pittsburgh, close to home.

When he was twenty, Curtis Martin had an encounter with God, and he promised that if God allowed him to live to age twenty-one, he would give his life to God and "do whatever You want me to do." After that encounter, Martin became convinced that God wanted him to live to help other people.

In 1995, when his college career came to an end, he was drafted by the New England Patriots. Bill Parcells, then coach of the Patriots, called Curtis to welcome him to the team. His family and pastor were with him when he took the call. After Curtis hung up the phone, he turned to his family and said, "Oh my gosh, I do *not* want to play football."

His pastor, Leroy Joseph, said, in effect, "Curtis, look at it this way—maybe football is something God is giving you so you can do good things for other people."

Curtis Martin later recalled that the moment his pastor said that, a light came on in his mind. Though he didn't have a passion for football, he did have a passion for God and for helping others. Martin realized that the football field could become his platform, his means of reaching and helping other people, and immediately upon joining the NFL he started a foundation to help disadvantaged kids and single mothers, funding it with 12 percent or more of every paycheck.

Martin was a football player who didn't like football, a running back who hated to run. Despite his lack of passion for football, Curtis Martin practiced hard and played hard, competing like a man possessed. He gained at least 1,000 yards in each of his first ten seasons in the NFL. His coaches and teammates all marveled at his intensity, his toughness, and his ability to play through injuries and pain. He outworked and outplayed his teammates, not out of passion for the game, but out of a passion to serve God. "The only way I was going to be successful at this game called football," he said, "is if I played for a purpose that was bigger than the game itself, because I know that the love for the game just wasn't in my heart."

After the 1997 season, Martin, a restricted free agent, signed with the New York Jets—one of two NFL teams he had previously vowed never to play for. "I looked at the Jets as the bottom of the barrel," he later recalled. But by this time, his old Patriots coach Bill Parcells had moved to the Jets, and Curtis Martin jumped at the chance to play for Parcells again.

Today, Curtis Martin acknowledges that football saved his life. The game lifted him out of a dangerous inner-city neighborhood in Pittsburgh and launched him on a stellar journey to the Football Hall of Fame. It gave him a platform and a vision for serving God and serving others—and that vision fueled his passion to excel in a game he didn't enjoy, with a team he didn't want to be on. His great talent intersected with an even greater passion, and he became an NFL legend.[8]

Sometimes our passion to excel comes from an unexpected place. As you look at your life, as you seek to identify your passion, be open to unexpected possibilities. You never know where your winning passion may come from.

Steps to Identifying Your Passion

I knew I had found my passion in life when I saw my first baseball game at Shibe Park in Philadelphia. Jack Ramsay found his passion in life the day his father fastened a basketball hoop to the wall of the barn. But for Condoleezza Rice and Curtis Martin, finding a passion to pursue in life was a difficult process of trial and error.

If you are trying to discover your passion in life, I have good news for you. There are practical steps you can take to focus your thinking, heighten your awareness, and help you identify a passion that will set you on the road to a successful, meaningful life. Here are the practical steps to discovering a passion that defines you:

1. *Ask yourself: "What is the work that feels like fun to me?"* When you are passionate about what you do, it doesn't seem like a chore. It feels like fun. You look forward to it because it's not an obligation, it's *play*.

Drew Houston, founder and CEO of Dropbox, gave the commencement address at his alma mater, MIT, in 2013. In his commencement address, he explained what it means to have such a passion for your work that work feels like fun. He used the analogy of a tennis ball:

> The happiest and most successful people I know don't just love what they do, they're obsessed with solving an important problem, something that matters to them. They remind me

> of a dog chasing a tennis ball. Their eyes go a little crazy, the leash snaps and they go bounding off, plowing through whatever gets in the way. . . . The problem is a lot of people don't find their tennis ball right away.
>
> It took me a while to get it, but the hardest-working people don't work hard because they're disciplined. They work hard because working on an exciting problem is fun. . . . It's not about pushing yourself; it's about finding your tennis ball, the thing that pulls you.[9]

What is your tennis ball? What pulls you? What kind of work would you enjoy doing even if no one paid you to do it? What kind of work feels like play to you? Once you are able to answer that question, you are well on your way to identifying your passion.

Ask yourself: "What would I do with my life if I didn't have to work for a living? What do I enjoy doing without being asked? What pastimes and pursuits make me lose track of time? What do I do that I hate to stop doing? What do I enjoy thinking about and reading about? What activities will I readily spend money on (for example, to read about it or travel for)? Is there a career path or business opportunity that would enable me to do that for a living?"

You might say, "I'm passionate about bird-watching." Can you get paid to bird-watch? Probably not. But you can get paid to do a job that is related to bird-watching.

With the appropriate degree, you could teach ornithology. You could become an environmental educator in a nonprofit organization or public school. You could be a research biologist, a science writer, a web developer, or a fund-raising specialist with, say, the Cornell Lab of Ornithology. You could become a field biologist with the US Fish and Wildlife Service.

There are private-sector jobs, too: bird-related publishing, building and selling bird-feeders, or selling specialized cameras and binoculars to the bird-watching community. You could become a professional bird photographer, illustrator, or author.

After you have identified potential career paths that match your passion, talk to people who are doing what you'd like to do. Ask them how they got started, what kind of education or training they needed, what talents and skills they brought to the table, and what sort of living one can expect to make.

Once you have found your "tennis ball," the career path that pulls you and excites you, a whole world of possibilities opens up. The only limits are the limits of your imagination.

2. *Ask yourself: "Is this idea, interest, or obsession big enough?"* One of Walt Disney's biggest dreams was Disneyland—perhaps the biggest gamble in business history. If Disneyland had failed, the Disney Studio would have folded. But Walt could see a future no one else envisioned. Walt once said, "If management likes my projects, I seriously question proceeding. If they disdain them totally, I proceed immediately." Walt had the stubborn perversity of genius, and he believed that if people around him approved of his ideas, then he simply wasn't dreaming big enough dreams.

3. *Ask yourself: "What was my childhood passion?"* Many of us fall in love with an idea, a sport, or a pursuit at an early age. For me, it was baseball. For Dr. Jack, it was basketball. For you, it might be collecting comic books or cycling with friends or drawing pictures or reading about dinosaurs or collecting butterflies or stargazing or playing music or

building model railroads. Most people who have a passion in childhood don't get over it by simply growing up. In fact, maintaining an interest in childhood passions enables us to feel like kids again, no matter how old and creaky our bones may be.

Is there a way to pursue your childhood passion and get paid for it? If so, you are the luckiest person on Planet Earth. You have a childhood passion that you can continue pursuing for as long as you live. In fact, you can probably list a dozen or more activities you enjoyed as a child and that you would still enjoy doing today. So go ahead, make a list. Your life's passion is likely somewhere on that list.

John Urschel is a six-foot-four, 312-pound guard with the NFL's Baltimore Ravens. He is also the coauthor of a peer-reviewed paper published in the *Journal of Computational Mathematics*. The paper is titled "A Cascadic Multigrid Algorithm for Computing the Fiedler Vector of Graph Laplacians." Urschel played college football at Penn State, where he earned his bachelor's and master's degrees in mathematics. In 2013 he won the William V. Campbell Award (sometimes called the "Academic Heisman"). During the NFL off-season, he is pursuing a PhD in mathematics from MIT.

Which is his overriding passion—football or mathematics? During the season, he is totally focused on football. But when he's doing math, he's all about the math. When working on mathematical problems, he says, "I feel a lot like I feel before a game. Nerves are naturally high, feeding off of uncertainty." He doesn't feel he has to choose between his two great passions, but can alternate between the two. "I can't think of anything I'd rather be doing," he says, "than playing in the NFL and getting my PhD in math from MIT. I've always aspired to do both."[10] (Though I normally recommend you choose one passion and pursue it with a single-minded focus, if you can juggle two passions side by side as John Urschel does, then more power to you.)

Urschel's passion for math goes back long before his passion for football. "I didn't start playing football until high school," he says. "Math is something I've done since I can remember. I'm very passionate about math—it's something I've been in love with for a very, very long time."[11]

John Urschel's childhood passion for math is still his passion today. What is your childhood passion? What if the passion that excited you as a child could become your bread-and-butter career today?

4. *Ask yourself: "At the end of my life, what do I want to leave as my legacy?"* How would you like to be remembered twenty or fifty years from now? What goals would you like to accomplish to define the life you lived? If you can answer those questions, you'll have a profound insight into your passion.

Take a piece of paper and write down your answer to those questions. Feel free to brainstorm and write down a number of different answers, then choose the most important one. Try to sum up the goal of your life in one brief statement.

Why keep it brief and simple? Because many of us are tempted to say we are "passionate" about a great many things—our faith, our families, our careers, our friends, our pets, our hobbies, and on and on. If you are passionate about everything, you are not truly passionate about anything. You just have a lot of interests. I believe it's a huge mistake to try to focus on too many things at once. While it's fine to have many interests, if you're intent on finding your sweet spot, you should focus on one great passion.

Journalist Clare Boothe Luce went to the White House and interviewed President John F. Kennedy soon after he was inaugurated. She was concerned that the ambitious young president might try to accomplish too much too soon—and in the process, he'd lose his sense of focus and purpose. During their conversation, Luce told Kennedy, "A great man is a sentence." In other words, people are more likely to follow a leader whose great passion can be summed up in a clear, concise statement. Journalist Warren Berger offers this example of how a great leader can be defined in a sentence: "Abraham Lincoln preserved the union and freed the slaves."[12]

How would you summarize the passion of your life? Can you state it in a sentence? Obviously, no single sentence can sum up an entire human life—but every human being who aspires to a successful, meaningful life should have an overriding passion that motivates and defines his or her life. What is your sentence? What is your passion?

5. *Ask yourself: "What stirs my desire to right wrongs, serve others, and make the world a better place?"* The best use of our passion is to focus it on a purpose and a cause that is far greater than ourselves. If our passion is focused only on selfish pursuits—on our own comfort, financial gain, status, power, or fame—then we have set our sights too low. That's not passion. That's just selfish ambition.

That doesn't mean you can't be passionate about a career in business or music or writing. A passionate entrepreneur who builds a successful business is serving others by creating wealth, creating jobs, providing a service to the community, and creating value for partners, shareholders, and stakeholders. A passionate musical performer or author creates art and beauty that benefits all who are touched by it.

You don't have to take a vow of poverty in order to serve others and serve God. If you feel called to take such a vow, then by all means, answer the call. But God has given some people a gift or a talent for creating wealth along with a passion for sharing that wealth with people in need. If you have a passion to serve God and others, you are well on your way to a purposeful, successful life.

Howard Thurman was an influential African-American author and preacher who served as the first dean of Rankin Chapel at Howard University from 1932 to 1944. In 1944, he cofounded the Church for the Fellowship of All Peoples in San Francisco, the first racially integrated interdenominational church in America. The author of more than twenty books on religion and philosophy, Howard Thurman had a great influence on Dr. Martin Luther King Jr. and other civil rights leaders. He once said, "Don't ask yourself what the world needs. Ask yourself what makes you come alive, and go and do that, because what the world needs is people who have come alive."[13]

So live passionately to make the world a better place. Live passionately to serve God. Live passionately to improve the lives of children, meet the needs of the elderly, save the lives of the sick and hungry, and restore the lives of addicts and prisoners and lost, lonely people. Find a passion worth pursing for a lifetime—and you will truly come alive.

What is *your* passion? And how far will your passion take you?

Next, it's time to start honing your talents for a lifetime of success.

4

Focus Your Talent

> Talent alone won't make you a success. Neither will being in the right place at the right time, unless you are ready. The most important question is: "Are you ready?"
>
> **JOHNNY CARSON**, entertainer

POLITICAL COMMENTATOR Chris Matthews, the host of the MSNBC nightly talk show *Hardball with Chris Matthews*, recalls a lesson he learned from Jimmy Schuhl, one of his classmates in elementary school. Jimmy was the most popular boy in class and he excelled in sports. And Jimmy's success was no accident. He once explained to young Chris Matthews exactly how he went about developing his talent and making sure his talent was recognized by others.

Every afternoon, Jimmy would go to the playground in his neighborhood and he'd stand by the basketball court. He'd watch the older kids playing basketball, and whenever the ball went out of bounds, Jimmy would retrieve it and throw it back to the big kids. Eventually, one of the big kids would have to leave the game and go home for supper. That left the teams uneven, so someone would yell to Jimmy, "Hey you, kid, want to play?"

And Jimmy would play. By playing basketball with the big kids, he developed his skills, and the other kids recognized his talent. Chris Matthews learned an important life lesson from Jimmy's example:

> There's a false assumption out there that talent will always be recognized. Just get good at something and the world will beat a path to your door. Don't believe it. The world is not checking in with us to see what skills we've picked up, what idea we've concocted, what dreams we carry in our hearts. When a job opens up, whether it's in the chorus line or on the assembly line, it goes to the person standing there. It goes to the eager beaver the boss sees when he looks up from his work, the pint-sized kid standing at courtside waiting for one of the older boys to head home for dinner. "Hey, kid, wanna play?". . .
>
> This is the logic that motivated me in 1971 as I knocked on two hundred doors on Capitol Hill before getting my first job in politics. The more I study the careers of successful people the more I see this pattern.[1]

It's true. *Finding* our talent is not enough. To achieve our dreams and reach our goals of a rewarding, successful life, we have to make our talents *shine*, so they'll be noticed by others. Once you have identified your talent, it's time to *focus* that talent on the pursuit of your greatest passion and your most important goals.

Invest in Yourself, Invest in Your Talent

In a 2009 interview with ABC News, Warren Buffett—the most successful investor in history—offered some sage advice about investing in your talent. "Investing in yourself," he said, "is the best thing you can do." Why? Because every other investment you make is subject to forces beyond your control, including taxes and economic downturns. But, says Buffett, nobody can tax your talent or take it away from you. Your talent is "a tremendous asset that can return tenfold."[2]

That's sound investment advice. But how do we invest in our talent? How do we maximize the value of this all-important asset?

A few years ago, a journalist wrote a book in which he proposed a concept he called "The 10,000 Hour Rule." He suggested that 10,000 hours is the amount of practice time we must invest in our talent in order to achieve mastery. This suggestion is based on research by Anders Ericsson, a Florida State University psychologist who studies human performance—yet Ericsson himself says his research has been misinterpreted.

"You don't get benefits from mechanical repetition, but by adjusting your execution over and over to get closer to your goal," Ericsson explains.[3] In other words, mere repetition for 10,000 hours will not enable you to achieve mastery. You have to push yourself to learn and improve as you practice. For example, if you spend 10,000 hours practicing the wrong way to swing a golf club, you'll only become a master mistake-maker, not a master golfer.

Whether you invest ten hours or 10,000 hours in your talent, your investment will be wasted if you are not learning from each repetition and increasing your skill level. The true masters of any skill or talent continually challenge themselves and compete against themselves to elevate their performance to the next level. Great athletes, great entertainers, great authors, and great leaders are constantly trying to top themselves. They know that 10,000 hours is not some magical tipping point to mastery—it's the bare minimum. It's the starting block, not the finish line.

Lori Jean Smith is an immensely talented violinist who performs everything from classical to pop to sacred music. She has performed with such international singing stars as Andrea Bocelli, and she earns standing ovations in concert halls, music festivals, and churches across the country. I've known her for years, and I never cease to be amazed at her vibrant, energetic performances which involve not only the artistry of the violin, but movement, energy, and showmanship.

I recently asked her how she learned to focus her talent and become so skilled at her instrument. She said, "Have you heard of 'The 10,000 Hour Rule'? Well, I passed the 10,000-hour mark a long time ago. There's so much more to mastering a talent than practicing for 10,000 hours. It takes a lot of focus, and a lot of pushing yourself to continually improve, and to master increasingly more challenging skills. You need a competitive fire that compels you to compete against yourself and others."

"How did you get started on the violin?"

"When I was seven years old, my parents gave me a violin. I started playing, and I instantly fell in love with it. And I got pretty good at it. But then, when I got to junior high school—well, that's when everything gets weird. None of my friends were playing the violin, and it just wasn't considered cool—so I didn't want to do it anymore. Even worse, I didn't like my violin teacher, so I quit my lessons.

"But I came back to the violin when I was a junior in high school. I learned about a statewide competition and a national competition, and there's something about the thought of competing that ignited my passion. So I practiced intensely and I won the state of Florida competition, qualified for the nationals, and then finished second. And that made me mad—I didn't want to finish second, I wanted to *win*.

"As a senior, I was determined to go forward again. I got a great teacher, and I worked on my weaknesses. I won Florida again and I qualified for the nationals. I didn't win at the national level, but it didn't matter. My love of this instrument had become so strong that my passion took over and carried me through."

I have seen Lori Jean Smith perform many times, and I can tell you that her talent shouts at you from her violin, and her passion is contagious. I have been in the audience when the standing ovation went on for more than two full minutes.

How will you focus your talent on your goals of success? Take Lori's word for it: there's nothing magical about 10,000 hours. The power comes from the focus you bring to those hours, and from your willingness to push your talent to the limit, to compete against yourself and top yourself—again and again and again.

My all-time baseball hero, Ted Williams, would have laughed at the notion that 10,000 hours of practice produces mastery. Born and raised in San Diego, California, Ted played sandlot baseball from his earliest years, then played minor league baseball in the Pacific Coast League at age eighteen. He joined the Boston Red Sox at age twenty-one and played his entire major league baseball career as a left fielder with the team.

In a major league playing career that spanned four decades (interrupted by two military tours of duty), Ted Williams, the "Splendid Splinter," hit .344 with 521 home runs and 1,839 runs batted in. His slugging percentage of .634 is still second only to Babe Ruth's .690. He posted a .406 batting average in 1941, and was the last major leaguer to hit over .400 in a season.

A few years ago, during a stay in San Diego, I took the Ted Williams boyhood tour. I started at Ted's boyhood home at 4121 Utah Street—a modest but neatly trimmed white bungalow set back from the street behind some large shrubs. I stood and imagined Ted as an eight-year-old boy, passionate about baseball, running out his front door and down the walk, a ball and glove in one hand, a bat in the other. I pictured that tree-lined street as it must have been in the late 1920s, and I imagined myself following along as he ran south on Utah Street.

I turned left at Polk Avenue, and in my imagination I followed that little boy as he sprinted toward Idaho Street and the community park where he used to play sandlot ball with other neighborhood boys. The park is still there, and the once-open field where he spent hours and hours playing sandlot ball is now a chain-link-fenced diamond with chalk lines, a neatly mowed outfield, bleachers, and lights for night games. A sign on the backstop reads "Ted Williams Field." That's where it all began.

Ted's father was distant and uninvolved, and his mother was a busy Salvation Army volunteer who was rarely home. So Ted and his younger brother had to fend for themselves. You could usually find Ted at the park with his pals, practicing his hitting and fielding until it was too dark to see. I went out on Ted Williams Field and imagined how it must have been in Ted's day, before there were fences and bleachers. I was walking on the same dirt where my hero had run the bases after clobbering that ball out of sight. I wondered how many golden hours a young Ted Williams had spent on that hallowed patch of San Diego real estate.

Next, I got in my car and drove east on El Cajon Boulevard to the three-story, tile-roofed Herbert Hoover High School. There I visited the baseball field where Ted had spent many more hours honing his skills as a pitcher, outfielder, and slugger. Here was a young man with an intense passion for baseball, with nothing but free time, growing up in San Diego, where the temperature is an even 72 degrees all year round. He probably racked up his first 10,000 hours of practice by the time he was twelve or fourteen. By the time he was out of high school and playing in the minor leagues, he could have easily doubled that.

Ted joined the Red Sox in 1939, decades before the advent of batting cages and baseball pitching machines, so he paid college kids to come to Fenway Park and pitch to him. How many hours of practice do you suppose he accumulated during his early years plus his four decades in the major leagues? It's impossible to say, but there's no doubt that it was many multiples of 10,000 hours. And perhaps more important than the number of hours Ted spent was the level of passion, intensity, focus, and drive to excel he brought to those hours. He constantly challenged himself to improve his performance and elevate his game. He sought every tiny increment of advantage, even specifying the quantity of knotholes in the Northern White Ash wood he personally selected for his custom-made bats.

Take any phenomenal and wildly successful individual in any field of endeavor from sports to the performing arts to literature to leadership, and you'll find that greatness is not made in mere hours of repetition, but in an intense desire to continually top oneself and to transform raw talent into absolute mastery. Greatness has more to do with how you invest your hours than with accumulating a specific number of hours.

That's how you leverage your talent and achieve your goals. That's the pathway to mastery and lifelong success.

Our natural talent is embedded in the neural pathways of the brain. The purpose of investing hours and hours of practice is to strengthen our neural "circuitry" and build more nerve pathways for the talent or skill we possess. That means we must commit ourselves to challenging ourselves, not merely doing what comes easily over and over again. If we don't push ourselves to learn increasingly more difficult skills and processes, our level of improvement will be negligible.

We all have a tendency to settle for a "good enough" performance level instead of pushing ourselves to the level of exhaustion and pain, where real improvement takes place. We prefer to play it safe instead of taking increasingly greater risks for our talent. If we want to get the most out of the hours we spend practicing, it helps to get feedback from a coach or mentor who will challenge us to stretch ourselves, push ourselves, and focus more intensely. No matter what our field of endeavor, we can always profit from the encouragement, instruction, and yes, the occasional tail-kicking from a coach or mentor.

If you want to focus your talent on your dreams and goals, you must invest in your talent through practice, focus, hard work, perseverance, coaching, and mentoring. You must invest your hours well in order to reap the harvest of accomplishments and success.

The Tragedy of Unfulfilled Potential

Everybody has a talent. Most of us have many talents. In fact, the world is full of talented people who never accomplish anything. There are many reasons why, but one of the top reasons is that they don't know how to translate talent into achievement. They don't know how to focus their talent on their goals and dreams of success.

Perhaps a relative, a teacher, or a coach once came to you and said, "You have so much potential." When you heard that statement, did you take it as a compliment? Well, don't. It's not a compliment. Everybody has potential. Only those who learn to focus their talent will actually *reach* their potential. Those who never learn to focus their talent only *waste* their potential.

Journalist Pete Hamill commented on the perplexing enigma—and the heartbreaking tragedy—of wasted potential:

> The fulfillment of talent is one of the most enduring human mysteries. Nobody can truly explain why a mediocre baseball player can become a brilliant baseball manager. Nobody absolutely knows why a singer of enormous technique can't move an audience or why so many gifted actors don't become stars. At six, some children play the piano with the confidence of Mozart, and at twenty they are working as record store clerks. There were some splendid young painters in my art school classes; almost all have vanished. I've seen young writers arrive in New York, bursting with talent, full of swagger and hubris, and then witnessed their descent after a few seasons into permanent silence. In political clubs, I've met men and women with great political intelligence, wonderful gifts for oratory, and unusual clarity about issues; they didn't make it out of the assembly district. For thousands of talented writers, painters, dancers, athletes, politicians, and actors, talent simply wasn't enough.[4]

It's absolutely true. If you want to achieve a meaningful, successful life, merely possessing talent is not enough. By itself, talent is nothing but unfulfilled potential. In order to achieve great goals, talent must be focused, directed, and propelled toward a target. Unfocused talent is unfulfilled potential.

To focus your talent on a goal of success, begin with a strategy. Invest in your talent, prepare for your success. You can't simply wait to be discovered or to have doors of opportunity opened for you. People rarely achieve their dreams of success by accident. Achievements and accomplishments are the result of focused planning and preparation. Life is a Rubik's Cube, a complex puzzle made of moving parts that interact in complex ways. In order to solve the puzzle of life, you must begin with a strategy.

A Strategy for Focusing Your Talent

Here is my suggested strategy for focusing your talent on your most important life goals:

1. *Start with a vision.* Once you have identified your talent and your passion, you've got the building blocks for a vision of your future. Gordon D'Angelo defines vision as "the definable intention from which preparation is formed."[5] In other words, your vision is the image of your intended destination. Your vision illuminates the pathway and shows you what you must do, day by day, hour by hour, to get there.

A vision statement defines what you will become, and it defines what success looks like to you. Write down that vision in one or two sentences (to make it simple and memorable, I recommend you keep it to fifty words or less). Print your vision in large type on a sheet of paper, and post it prominently where you will see it every day. State it as a strong, uncompromising affirmation—not "I want to" or "I hope to," but *I will.* Let me suggest a few examples of vision statements.

A corporate CEO: "Over the next decade, my spouse and children will know I love them because I put my family before business. My employees, stakeholders, and customers will know that I lead with integrity, loyalty, compassion, and imagination—and our product will be in every home in America."

A teacher: "Ten years from now, I will be known as a teacher who made learning fun and exciting, who inspired a sense of wonder in my students, and who lifted every student to his or her full potential."

A writer: "I will publish at least one novel per year, and ten years from now, I will be a full-time, self-employed writer, earning a six-figure income while bringing excitement, entertainment, and life-changing ideas to my loyal readers."

A stay-at-home mom: "Ten years from now, my children will follow God with all their hearts, they will know I love them intensely, and they will amaze and inspire everyone around them by the way they love God and serve others."

Why is it important to have a vision of the future? Let me suggest three key reasons:

First, your vision keeps you focused on what is truly important. It wards off distractions and keeps you true to your greatest talent and deepest passion in life.

Second, your vision keeps you fired up. Every time you look at your vision of the future, it should fill you with energy and enthusiasm for meeting the challenges of each day. Andy Stanley, author of *Visioneering*, put it this way: "Vision evokes emotion. . . . A clear, focused vision actually allows us to experience ahead of time the emotions associated with our anticipated future. These emotions serve to reinforce our commitment to the vision. . . . The clearer the vision, the stronger the emotion."[6]

Sir Richard Branson, the billionaire founder of the Virgin Group of companies, often talks about vision as an essential ingredient of success. He has an overarching vision for all of his companies that he has expressed in three words: "People, Planet, and Profit." In short, he believes that it is not only possible but absolutely necessary that corporations put people and the planet first—and he believes corporations can do so while still earning healthy profits. Branson wants to completely change the way businesses, investors, and governments define success.

He explains, "I strongly believe that big business needs to play its role in supporting society for the greater good. . . . We all have a part to play, but I believe entrepreneurs will have a really significant role to play in bringing investment and commercial skills to help develop the new technologies needed to grow a post-carbon economy."[7]

Branson has a vision for impacting social problems and human need through his nonprofit organizations, Virgin Unite and The Carbon War Room. He wants to use entrepreneurial capitalism to find solutions to problems of war, injustice, global warming, and energy consumption.

Richard Branson is also pursuing his "People, Planet, and Profit" vision through more than four hundred companies he has created in fields ranging from entertainment to medical technology to energy production. Branson founded his first business at age sixteen—a successful youth-culture magazine. At twenty-two, he founded a chain of record stores, Virgin Records, which later became a highly successful recording label. At thirty-four, he founded Virgin Atlantic Airways.

In 2004 he created his most visionary company of all, Virgin Galactic, which embodies Branson's vision of our future in space. He is committed to inventing a new industry, space tourism, under the auspices of Virgin Galactic. In fact, he plans to be aboard for the company's maiden voyage, and intends to bring his parents (both in their nineties), his children, physicist Stephen Hawking, actor William Shatner (*Star Trek*'s Captain Kirk), and other big names for Virgin Galactic's first suborbital passenger flight. And that's just the beginning.

Branson also plans to construct a space hotel in orbit to facilitate tourism to the moon and beyond. And he envisions using his SpaceShipTwo aerospace craft to shuttle passengers on transcontinental flights at low-orbital altitudes. The flights would last about half an hour, and would produce far less pollution than jet aircraft.[8] Branson once said, "A successful business isn't the product or service it sells, its supply chain or its corporate culture. It is a group of people bound together by a common purpose and vision."[9] Sir Richard Branson's vision fires him up to reach for the stars.

Third, vision helps you finish. It keeps you going through times of opposition and adversity, and draws you to your destination. As Steve Jobs once said, "If you are working on something exciting that you really care about, you don't have to be pushed. The vision pulls you."[10]

Stay focused, stay fired up, and finish strong. Keep your vision always in front of you, and let your vision pull you toward your dream of success.

2. *Sacrifice and work hard every day to turn your vision into reality*. "You can do almost anything you want in life, as long as you are willing to accept the sacrifices involved in getting there," said athlete-entrepreneur Dave McGillivray, founder of Dave McGillivray Sports Enterprises.[11]

And Packers legend Bart Starr quoted coach Vince Lombardi as telling the team, "If you give anything less than what you have within you at any time, regardless of the situation, regardless of the consequences, you're cheating yourself, you're cheating your teammates, you're cheating professional football, and you're cheating the fans who made the game what it is today for you. But most of all, you're cheating your Maker who gave you that God-given talent with which to succeed."[12]

Kristen Lamb is the author of *Rise of the Machines* and *We Are Not Alone*. After working for a dozen years as a writer and editor, she observed, "Talent is highly overrated. . . . I constantly meet writers more talented than I am, but I know they won't make it despite their superior abilities. Why? Because they're lazy."

Lamb tells the story of a former boyfriend who had "an IQ so high it couldn't be accurately measured." She met him when she was going to college while working in sales and also teaching jujitsu. Her boyfriend attended the class, and for the first three months he would arrive early and stay late. But then his attendance waned, and he started making excuses. Finally he quit jujitsu and took up kung fu.

Kristen Lamb's boyfriend also bailed out on his master's program in political science, opting instead to pursue a career in police work. At first, Lamb thought that he was a man of many interests, trying to find his passion in life. But then it occurred to her that he was just too lazy to stick with one thing very long.

One day he announced he wanted to become a writer. Since Lamb was trying to build a career in writing, he asked her to help him achieve his goal. "I was young and dumb and tried to encourage his genius," she said, "because he was so stinkin' smart it was spooky and that was what I loved about him."

But try as she might to encourage his writing, he always offered excuses for not working and not accomplishing anything. He'd claim he needed "the right desk lamp from IKEA, a sharper pencil, a faster computer, more free time, or a house by the sea."

Eventually, Lamb and her boyfriend parted ways. Years later, she happened to run into him in a store, and he asked, "Are you still in sales?"

"No, I left the corporate world. I'm an author now. I write full-time."

"I want to be an author," he said, adding that he was held back by his ADD (attention deficit disorder). "Maybe you can help me."

Lamb wasn't persuaded by his excuses. "No," she said, "you don't have ADD. You lack maturity and discipline."[13]

Like any other talent-based pursuit in life, success in writing is a matter of sacrifice, hard work, and self-discipline. In order to focus your talent and achieve success, you must overcome excuses, procrastination, and the natural human tendency to laziness. All the talent in the world can achieve nothing without a commitment to hard work.

3. *Take risks.* English writer and churchman Sydney Smith said, "A great deal of talent is lost to the world for want of a little courage." This word *courage* is one of the noblest, most inspiring words in our language. It comes from the Old French *corage* by way of the Latin word *cor*, meaning "heart." For centuries, people have understood that courage speaks of the state of our hearts, the essential quality found at the core of our being. People of courage are people who take risks.

Courage is not the absence of fear, but the will to do the right thing in spite of our fear. As Ralph Waldo Emerson said, "Do the thing you fear, and the death of fear is certain." Heroes and cowards both know fear. The difference is that cowards run from fear while heroes run toward it. People of courage seize opportunities, challenge the status quo, accept responsibility for failures, and keep moving toward their goals. People of courage stand firm for their values, principles, and goals instead of taking the easy path of compromise. There is no success without courage, because success requires investment, and investment entails risk.

To invest in yourself, you must put your talent at risk. Your talent is one of your most valuable assets. To grow that asset, to realize a return on investment, be willing to bet on yourself, to bet on your talent. Be willing to take risks—not foolish gambles, but prudent, well-planned risks.

Tania Modic is a founding partner and chief investment officer of Western Investments Capital, LLC. A graduate of the University of Southern California, she gave the commencement address to the USC Marshal Business School, telling the graduating class of 1996, "You are responsible for the shareholder value of 'you.com.' You are the sole stockholder."[14]

Fresh out of college, Tania Modic landed her first job with an international bank. Her title was "assistant marketing development officer," even though there was no marketing development officer to assist. It was a boring job and provided no challenges for her talent. It also provided little potential for advancement. So Modic decided to make a risky investment in her talent. Having assisted many senior people in the bank, she knew that she had the talent and ability to do their jobs. But she would never get a chance to advance unless she could get the attention of top management.

So Tania Modic came up with a plan to use her vacation time for a trip to New York. There she would call on accounts that her immediate superiors had neglected, and she would try to persuade them to bring their business back to the bank. Modic knew that if she succeeded, her immediate superiors would resent it. They'd say, "This upstart new hire is making me look bad!" She calculated the odds of various outcomes for her plan. She estimated she had a 70 percent chance of succeeding in bringing back lost business—so far, so good. And she figured she had a 60 percent chance of raising her visibility and getting noticed by management—also good. But she estimated that she had a 100 percent chance of angering her immediate superiors and a 50 percent chance of getting fired.

Weighing the risks versus the benefits, she decided these were acceptable odds. So she went to New York and persuaded a number of clients to return to the bank. As she expected, some people were miffed—but her success insulated her from retaliation. Senior management took notice of the lucrative business she had brought to the bank, and she was rewarded with praise and a promotion.[15]

In her USC commencement address, Tania Modic recalled, "When I was kicked out of Catholic grammar school, the nun told my mother, 'I don't know if this is the most gifted child or if she needs professional help.' My husband, hearing this story years later, said, 'Well, now we know, don't we?'"[16] Indeed we do. Tania Modic is gifted with a special talent—a talent called courage. She is willing to take risks to invest in herself and her talent. And that is why she succeeds.

Courageously live your life as an experiment. In science, experiments don't always yield the results we expect. Sometimes the results are disappointing. Sometimes experiments yield answers, insights, and benefits we never imagined. So be daring. Live boldly. Take risks. Try new experiences. Meet new people. Accept new challenges. Invest in your talent at every opportunity.

Author and entrepreneur Faisal Hoque puts it this way: "When success isn't guaranteed, or even likely, the risk can seem too great—especially when it's ourselves we're betting on. There's comfort in the known. But that comfort limits our potential for growth. And it can hold us back from discovering who we truly are."[17]

Discover yourself, focus your talent, and take risks to achieve your goals.

4. *Never give up.* To focus your talent on your goals, persevere through obstacles, opposition, and even failure. Setbacks and failures are inevitable. Don't let them define you. Instead of saying, "I'm a failure," say, "That attempt failed, which means I discovered what works and what doesn't. Time to get up and try again." Every time you push past setbacks and failures, you gain strength, knowledge, and confidence that will serve you well in the future.

Someone once said that perseverance is a talent—and I agree. It may well be the most important talent you have. So go easy on yourself when you fail. Be patient when things don't come as quickly as you'd like. Don't try to consume the meal of your life in a single bite—take it gradually, in manageable bites, confident that all of the changes you are making in your life day by day will add up to a huge difference when you reach your goal.

Whenever you feel frustrated by setbacks or failures, ask yourself, "What one thing can I do today that will move me closer to my ultimate goal?" Once you have answered that question, do it—and keep moving forward.

5. *Focus your talent by maintaining your curiosity and a commitment to continuous learning.* Feed your inquiring mind with good books and other informative media. Listen and learn—then use what you have learned to multiply your skills and magnify your talent.

Educator Deborah Morrison says we should never stop wondering, reading, and learning. Writing in *Fast Company*, she observes, "Curiosity is key. We find that directly developing this skill . . . opens doors to bigger thinking and investment." Curiosity in itself is a kind of talent, and people who are curious about the world ("How does that work? Who does this affect? Why why why?") are better able to acquire "hybrid skills." They experience the "joy of connection" and they gain an interdisciplinary understanding of how the world works. A thirst for learning—a curiosity about how people, technology, and society function—helps to foster our talent and creativity, building "a way of thinking for a lifetime."[18]

6. *Remain humble.* Talented people are easily tempted to feel more important and more entitled than other people, simply because of their talent. They began to think of their leadership role as a right—and that sometimes causes them to treat other people as "inferiors."

Supermodel Kim Alexis recalls an incident that occurred when she was having dinner with some wealthy friends in Florida. During the meal, the waiter came and refilled everyone's water glass. As the waiter filled hers, Kim said, "Thank you." It was not a big deal to her—she always thanks those who do something kind for her.

After the waiter left, the man across from her said, "You don't have to thank those people! You're better than they are."

Kim was shocked. "God made us all," she said. "The waiter is just as important as I am. It's just common courtesy to say thank you."

Her dinner companion was baffled. "Really, Kim! Don't you understand? That guy gets paid minimum wage to fill people's water glasses. You're on the cover of *Vogue* and *Sports Illustrated*! You've done so much more than people like that! Of course you're better than they are!"[19]

Kim later recalled, "That conversation was a real eye-opener to me." Until that moment, it had never occurred to her that some people considered themselves better than others. Kim Alexis has a talent that enabled her to make a good living gracing the covers of magazines—yet she never let her talent go to her head. She never let her talent as a supermodel make her feel superior, self-important, or entitled. No matter what your talent may be, remain humble.

As legendary UCLA Bruins basketball coach John Wooden once said, "Talent is God-given. Be humble. Fame is man-given. Be grateful. Conceit is self-given. Be careful."[20]

Once you have begun to focus your talent on achieving your most important goals in life, you begin to realize that talent is only one side of the equation. You still must learn how to focus your passion on your goals in order to achieve the life you dream of. That is what we will discover next.

5

Focus Your Passion

> Passion is another word for enthusiasm, which translates into energy, which in turn produces action. The more passion and energy you have, the more things you're likely to get done in the course of a day or a week or year—and the better off you and your organization will be.
>
> **JIM CALHOUN**, college basketball coach

JIM HENSON GREW UP in Mississippi and Maryland, and he spent many happy hours by the family radio, listening to ventriloquist Edgar Bergen entertain audiences with his wisecracking puppets Charlie McCarthy and Mortimer Snerd. In 1950, when the Henson family bought a TV set, fourteen-year-old Jim Henson became enthralled with a televised puppet show, *Kukla, Fran and Ollie*, created by puppeteer Burr Tillstrom. The show featured puppets with believable personalities and literate humor that was based on relationships between characters rather than slapstick. *Kukla, Fran and Ollie* exerted an enormous influence on the imagination of young Jim Henson.

Soon, Henson was creating his own puppets and marionettes, which he used to put on children's shows. He taught himself the art of puppetry from library books. As a high school senior, he convinced a local CBS television station to hire him and a friend to create a children's show featuring marionettes. The show didn't last long, but it did catch the eye of a producer at a rival NBC television station—and Jim Henson and his puppets were soon on the air again.

At the University of Maryland, he studied stage design and costuming, which aided him in the creation of his puppets. There he also met Jane Nebel, who would soon become his business partner and wife. He experimented and pioneered many new techniques for making more expressive and believable puppets—and by the mid-1950s, he was referring to his puppets as "Muppets."

Henson's biographer, Brian Jay Jones, described Jim Henson and his wife as two people fused together by intense passions. "Jim and Jane's relationship," he wrote, "was based on passion—passion for art, for performance, and for each other—but it was more a business proposal than a marriage proposal."[1]

While still in their early twenties, Jim and Jane Henson worked together to create Muppets segments for NBC's *Tonight Show* starring Steve Allen. They also created Muppet commercials, and quickly developed a reputation for producing commercials that were funnier and more eye-catching than the programs they appeared on. In 1958, Jim and Jane formed Muppets, Inc., and during the 1960s, Jim Henson's Muppets, starring the piano-playing dog Rowlf, made regular appearances on Jimmy Dean's ABC television variety show.

In 1968, the Children's Television Workshop hired Jim Henson to help create a new program for public television called *Sesame Street*. His goal was to hold the attention of children and educate them without letting them know they were learning. Soon after the show hit the airwaves, characters such as Bert and Ernie, Cookie Monster, and Big Bird became household names.

One of Jim Henson's closest friends and top puppeteers, Frank Oz, remembered Henson as a man of intense passion for his work. "He was quiet and unassuming when you met him," Oz said, "but he also had this steely determination to succeed. That enabled him to create more popular characters than anyone since Walt Disney."[2] In spite of being so driven, Henson had a reputation as a kind and gentle leader who never raised his voice and never showed disrespect to anyone. Sadly, Henson died at the age of fifty-three.

In 2005, Henson's daughter Cheryl, president of the Jim Henson Foundation, assembled a book of her father's wisdom called *It's Not Easy Being Green*. In that book, Jim Henson expressed the passion for his work that had motivated and inspired him throughout his career:

> I don't resent working long hours. I shouldn't—I'm the one who set up my life this way. I love to work. It's the thing that I get the most satisfaction out of—and probably what I do best. Not that I don't enjoy days off. I love vacations and loafing around. But I think much of the world has the wrong idea

> of working. It's one of the good things in life. The feeling of accomplishment is more real and satisfying than finishing a good meal—or looking at one's accumulated wealth.[3]

Because of Jim Henson's great passion for his work—a passion that went all the way back to his childhood, sitting by the radio, laughing with Charlie McCarthy and Mortimer Snerd—he never resented work. His work was a labor of love. Jim Henson's life was all too short—but by living passionately, he packed many lifetimes worth of achievement into his brief span of fifty-three years. The world is richer and happier because Jim Henson and all his Muppet friends were in it.

Looking back on Henson's life, author David Zahl reflected, "Henson was, by all accounts, a bit of a saint. Read any biography of the man, and you will walk away almost suspicious of his overwhelming decency and personal integration, his unfailing optimism and boundless energy. What made the biggest impression on those around him was apparently not his astounding creativity, but the passionate and compassionate way he lived his life."[4]

And filmmaker Robert Jones called Jim Henson "a man on a mission—with a passionate desire to make a positive difference in the world. He believed that entertainment—especially film and television—could be used as a force for good. . . . Using his talent as an entertainer, Henson wanted to change attitudes, change lives, and—more than anything—make people laugh."[5]

Jim Henson discovered his passion at an early age, and he focused his passion on dreams of bringing joy and laughter to millions. That's why he succeeded—and that's why he's a role model for you and me.

A Passionate Perspective

In the Ashmolean Museum in Oxford, England, there's an oil painting by the Italian Renaissance master Paolo Uccello. Painted around 1470, it is entitled *The Hunt in the Forest*. The painting makes a startling impression the moment you see it. The scene is a dark forest at nightfall. Beneath a dark sky and a shadowy canopy of trees, we see a large hunting party—more than a dozen hunters on horseback, arrayed in brightly colored garments of red, orange, and blue, plus attendants carrying staves, and more than two dozen hunting hounds. The trees, the hounds, the horses, and the riders all diminish in perspective as they recede into the distance. All the figures—the men, the horses, and the hounds—are looking toward a single point in the distance at the center of the canvas. They are looking toward the object of the hunt, which we assume is a stag, hidden behind the trees.

What is the historic significance of this painting? It is one of the early experiments by Paolo Uccello using a new technique called "perspective." Before Uccello's use of perspective, almost all paintings appeared flat and two-dimensional. Figures in the distance were proportionally the same size as figures in the foreground. There was no sense of depth, no sense of distant objects receding from us in a realistic perspective.

Paolo Uccello was more than a painter—he was a trained mathematician. He applied principles of mathematics to his drawings and paintings. He would start with a vanishing point and draw lines of perspective in order to create a sense of depth. While most other painters of his era were simply trying to tell a story through their paintings, Uccello was reaching for visual realism.

Sixteenth-century painter Giorgio Vasari profiled Paolo Uccello in his book *Lives of the Most Excellent Painters, Sculptors, and Architects* (1550), in which he wrote that Paolo Uccello was so passionate about perspective that he left behind "chests full of drawings" and that he "[gave] himself up to perspective, and remained poor and obscure until his death."

Vasari also records this glimpse into Paolo Uccello's passion for this new painting technique called perspective: "His wife used to say that Paolo would sit studying perspective all night, and when she called him to come to bed he would answer, 'Oh, what a sweet thing this perspective is!'"[6]

What does the success intersection look like? It looks like a fifteenth-century Italian painter, Paolo Uccello, obsessed with a completely new and original way of painting. It looks like a man filling wooden chests with drawing after drawing, focusing his talent as he pursues his new vision of reality. When our talent intersects with our greatest passion, success will happen. We may even discover an entirely new perspective on reality.

A Passion to Be the Best

In 1999, I wrote my autobiography, published by Revell (which published an updated and expanded version in 2014). My editors suggested the title for the book: *Ahead of the Game: The Pat Williams Story*. I liked the title and still do. My original title was *A Passion for Distinction*. The publisher's title was undoubtedly a more marketable title, but I think my original title summed up the theme of my life in four words. From my boyhood, through my college years, throughout my career, and to this very day, I have been driven and motivated by a passion for distinction, a passion for excellence in everything I do. In my early years, I had a passion for distinction in sports. Over time, I developed new interests—sports broadcasting, sports management, leadership, speaking, and writing—but dominating and uniting all these interests is a passion for excellence, for distinction. My life has been blessed, and I truly do feel that, by God's grace, I'm "ahead of the game"—yet I still believe it's my passion for distinction that captures the essence of my life.

Another author whose book title summed up his life was the late Kirby Puckett, who played his entire twelve-year major league baseball career as a center fielder for the Minnesota Twins. His book, published in 1993, was called *I Love This Game!*—and yes, the exclamation point was part of the title. Kirby Puckett always talked in exclamation points.

In *Confessions of a Baseball Purist*, sportscaster Jon Miller talked about Kirby Puckett's passion for living each day to the fullest, and for playing the game he loved so much:

> When Kirby was playing for the Twins and I'd run into him at the ballpark, we'd trade smiles, shake hands, and invariably would begin a conversation that went something like this:
>
> Me: "Kirby, how're you doing, man?"
>
> Kirby: "Fantastic, Mill." . . .
>
> Me: "Fantastic again? You were fantastic last month. You were fantastic last year. Kirby, how can you always be fantastic?"

Kirby: "C'mon Mill, you know that every day I put on this uniform is a fantastic day!"

Every time. And every time, I knew that Kirby meant it.[7]

Another baseball star with a genuine passion for the game is Cal Ripken Jr., who played twenty-one seasons with the Baltimore Orioles, 1981 to 2001. Playing shortstop and third base, Ripken—nicknamed "the Iron Man"—compiled a career record of 3,184 hits, 431 home runs, and 1,695 runs batted in. He was inducted into the Baseball Hall of Fame in 2007, his first year of eligibility. On September 6, 1995, he broke the record for consecutive games played when he started his 2,131st consecutive game. He ended his seventeen-year streak at 2,632 games in 1998.

Cal Jr.'s passion for the game has driven him to do all the little things on a daily basis that add up to a long and distinguished athletic career—taking care of his health and conditioning, making sure he's ready to play at every game, and making sure he is serious about competing hard and winning. He focused his talent. He once said, "I ran into a lot of players toward the end of their careers and I would ask do you have any regrets. Most of them said I wish I would have taken care of myself better, I wish I had played more, I wish I had taken it more seriously. Those are the three things I definitely will not say when I'm done."[8]

Ripken gives much of the credit for his achievements to his father, Cal Sr., a longtime player and coach with the Orioles organization who passed away in 1999. In the foreword to his father's book *The Ripken Way: A Manual for Baseball and Life*, Cal Jr. writes:

> You don't set out to do something like the Streak. It certainly wasn't a goal of mine. Dad taught me how to play the game, and there's a certain expectation from that approach, what your responsibilities are. Executing that approach means coming to the ballpark and saying to your manager, I'm ready to play for you. And if you want to put me in there, it's my job to give you everything I have.
>
> The Streak was born because my father taught me to come to the ballpark with a desire and a passion to play.[9]

In 2015, I achieved a goal I had been chasing for a number of years—I wrote a book called *Vince Lombardi on Leadership: Life Lessons from a Five-Time NFL Championship Coach*. In the course of researching that book, I spoke with every living human being I could track down who had ever known Coach Lombardi, going all the way back to his high school coaching days and his years as an assistant to coach Red Blaik at the Military Academy at West Point. Again and again, as I interviewed players, sports writers, and even the lady in charge of the Green Bay Packers cheerleading squad, I was impressed to hear that the one characteristic that defined Coach Lombardi was *passion*.

Jerry Kramer was an offensive guard for the Packers from 1958 to 1968. He recalls Coach Lombardi as a man driven by passion. "He was incredibly demanding. He was a driven kind of human. He once told me, 'I have a burning incandescence in my gut.' It propelled him."

It was Lombardi's passion for winning, for being the best, that motivated him to demand the utmost from his Packers. "He worked us harder than any team in the business at that time," Kramer recalls. "[Defensive tackle] Dave Hanner of Arkansas was a perfect example. For five days he would spend mornings at practice and afternoons in the hospital getting an IV. There were guys losing consciousness, passing out and vomiting. That was the age when you didn't take fluids. . . . It was intense."[10]

In *What It Takes to Be #1*, Coach Lombardi's son, Vince Jr., wrote about the passion that drove him to be the best in his profession, coaching the best team in the league:

> Passion is any emotion that moves you. It can be love, hate, enthusiasm, intensity, or zeal. Lombardi was once described by a friend as having the "zeal of a missionary." And although the Packers held a special place in his heart, his passion extended into all corners of his life. . . .
>
> His enthusiasm overflowed. It was a passion that could be neither corralled nor fended off. "If you said 'Good morning' to him in the right way," said Giants owner Wellington Mara, "you could bring tears to his eyes." His emotional ups and downs as an assistant coach with the Giants earned him a nickname: "Mr. Hi-Lo." A colleague once criticized him for getting worked up over what appeared to be a minor football matter. Lombardi said, in response, "If you can't get emotional about what you believe in your heart, you're in the wrong business."[11]

Vince Jr. went on to offer a quotation from his father, in which Coach Lombardi described his passion for winning in his own words: "I'm an emotional man. I cry. I cried when we won the Super Bowl, and I cried when I left Green Bay. Now, I'm not ashamed of crying. Football's an emotional game. You can't be a cold fish and go out and coach. If you're going to be involved in it, you gotta take your emotions with you, mister."[12]

A Strategy for Focusing Your Passion

Michael Mink is a writer and editor with *Investor's Business Daily*. I have gotten to know Michael, and he has been my writing partner on several books. He has written more than five hundred articles for *IBD*, mostly on leadership and success. I once asked him, "Based on all the study and writing you've done about great people in business, the military, sports, and science, what one trait have you observed that all high-achieving people have in common?"

Without hesitation, he said, "Passion is the common denominator. They all had an intense passion for their work and their goals."

Talent alone is not enough to take you to your vision of a successful and meaningful life. You must focus that talent on one overriding passion—and you must use that vision of success to harness the power of passion to keep you focused on your goals. Let me suggest some ways to focus your passion on those goals:

1. *Narrow the focus of your passion.* No one can be passionate about a hundred things, or even ten things, at once. To achieve your goals, you must narrow your focus and discard any so-called "passions" that distract you from your one essential passion. Choose one passion, one objective, and pour all of your enthusiasm and talent into a single-minded pursuit of that goal.

When Larry Page was a graduate student at Stanford, he didn't know what he wanted to do with his life. "I had about ten different ideas of things I wanted to do," he recalls, "and one of them was to look at the link structure of the [World

Wide Web]. My advisor, Terry Winograd, picked that one out and said, 'Well, that one seems like a really good idea.'"

Page focused on that concept and made it the basis for a new approach to internet search engines. In 1998, Page cofounded (with Sergey Brin) a company called Google (I'm sure you've heard of it). The average computer user conducts dozens of Google searches every day. You type in your search term, and your results pop up in roughly half a second. [13]

In 2014, *Bloomberg* listed Larry Page as the seventeenth richest person in the world; the following year, *Forbes* called Google "the most influential company of the digital era."

When you focus on one passion, you know exactly where you should focus your talent and energies. Your passion enables you to focus on what you do best, and discover what your own contributions to the world will be. Peter G. Peterson, senior chairman of the Blackstone Group, a financial services company, studied economics under the Nobel Prize-winning economist Milton Friedman at the University of Chicago Graduate School of Business. Friedman had a huge impact on Peterson's thinking. "He worshipped free markets and was also a powerful advocate of Adam Smith's concept of comparative advantage: focus on those things you do better than others. That has been enormously helpful in defining our business strategies."

Peterson recalls that, in 1985, when he and Steve Schwarzman founded the Blackstone Group, their advisors told them to specialize in acquiring companies through hostile leveraged buyouts. Peterson and Schwarzman rejected that advice. "We felt that our advantage was that we were on friendly terms with many American CEOs and boards," Peterson explained. "We took the contrarian position. We would only do strictly friendly investments. As a result, so-called corporate partnerships have become a major foundation—and a very profitable contribution—to our business."[14]

As Walker Percy said, "Lucky is the man who does not secretly believe that every possibility is open to him."[15]

Before Steve Jobs cofounded Apple, he lived on a farm, a hippie commune run by a friend. Jobs worked in the commune's apple orchard (which later inspired the computer company's name). He pruned trees and ran the commune's cider press. Jobs later said that while pruning trees to make them more productive, he realized that pruning the number of ideas or products a company focuses on can make a company more productive.

Jobs and his business partner, Steve Wozniak, cofounded Apple in 1976. The company's most successful product at that time was the Apple II personal computer. As CEO of the company, Jobs made sure that Apple focused on doing a few things exceptionally well.

After a bitter power struggle, Steve Jobs was forced out of Apple in 1985. He founded NeXT, a computer platform development company. He also funded a spinoff computer graphics division of the George Lucas motion picture company Lucasfilm. That spinoff company became Pixar, the computer animation company that produced *Toy Story* and other hit films.

Following Jobs's departure, Apple began diversifying its product lines—and by 1997, the company was on the verge of bankruptcy. Apple brought Jobs back into the company by purchasing NeXT. One of Steve Jobs's first acts as the returning CEO was to prune the number of products Apple produced from 350 to 10. Once Apple returned to its original philosophy of doing a few things exceptionally well, the company was back on the path to global success.

Nike CEO Mark Parker once asked Steve Jobs if he had any advice on making Nike more successful. Without hesitation, Jobs replied, "Just one thing. Nike makes some of the best products in the world. Products that you lust after. But you also make a lot of crap. Just get rid of the crappy stuff and focus on the good stuff."

Parker laughed, thinking Jobs was joking. When Jobs didn't laugh, Parker realized the Apple CEO was dead serious. "He was absolutely right," Parker later recalled. "We had to edit." In other words, Nike needed to prune away product lines that were distractions from the company's central purpose and passion.

As Steve Jobs once said, "People think focus means saying yes to the thing you've got to focus on. But that's not what it means at all. It means saying no to the hundred other good ideas that there are. You have to pick carefully. I'm actually as proud of the things we haven't done as the things we have done. Innovation is saying 'no' to a thousand things."[16]

To be successful, don't get carried away with every new idea, new opportunity, or new possibility that comes along. Stay true to your passion.

2. *Seek out mentors who encourage your passion.* Nineteen-year-old tennis player Pete Sampras shocked the world by becoming the youngest men's champion at the 1990 US Open. It takes more than talent to rock the tennis world the way Pete Sampras did—and he had what it took. Sampras demonstrated a depth of poise, mental toughness, and emotional intensity far beyond his years. Where did all that prowess

come from? How did he achieve greatness at such an early age?

Answer: he learned it from his mentors.

Pete Sampras grew up playing tennis from an early age in Rancho Palos Verdes, California. Tennis was his passion. While in high school, Sampras decided that, in order to achieve his dreams and goals, he needed to be mentored by the best. So, at age seventeen, Sampras contacted Czech tennis star Ivan Lendl, then the top professional tennis player in the world. Lendl let Sampras stay at his home in Connecticut to learn by observing.

Sampras recalled, "Without saying anything, [Lendl] showed me what it takes to be a champion, how organized he was, how focused he was. That certainly was a good experience for me." Perhaps the most important influence Lendl had on Sampras was through the example of his intense work ethic, which included grueling thirty-mile bicycle rides every day to build his endurance.

Passionately eager to learn and grow, Pete Sampras sought out other tennis greats as his mentors and role models, including tennis pro Jim Courier and coach Tim Gullikson. "You take little pieces of the puzzle from everyone," he said. Pete Sampras accelerated his rise to the top by seeking out mentors who taught him the shortcuts that propelled him to his dreams. His mentors helped him leverage his intense passion into stratospheric heights of success.[17]

Milan-born Andrea Guerra is the former CEO of Luxottica SpA, the world's largest maker of eyewear. In 2004, he was named on the *Financial Times* list of 25 Business Stars. His first position in the business world was with the Marriott hotel chain. There his supervisor gave him an excellent piece of advice: "In your first years of business life, you shouldn't go chasing after fancy titles, but try to find people who can teach you something."[18]

Seek out mentors who can encourage and channel your passion.

3. *Focus your passion by doing, not dabbling.* The nineteenth-century preacher Dwight L. Moody noted that the apostle Paul once said, "This one thing I do,"[19] but most people say instead, "These fifty things I dabble in." To focus your passion on your goals of success, you must be a doer, not a dabbler. Doers are busy accomplishing their goals while dabblers are still waiting to get started.

Walt Disney accomplished amazing things because he was a doer, not a dabbler. Neal Gabler, in *Walt Disney: The Triumph of the American Imagination*, observed, "Walt Disney seldom dabbled. Everyone who knew him remarked on his intensity; when something intrigued him, he focused himself entirely as if it were the only thing that mattered."[20] And Walt himself explained how he focused his passion: "You get an idea, and you just can't wait. Once you've started, then you're in there with the punches flying. There's plenty of trouble, but you can handle it. You can't back out. It gets you down once in a while, but it's exciting. Our whole business is exciting."[21]

4. *Focus on your passion, not on making money.* Over the years, many people have asked me what they should do to become successful. So I ask them, "What do you mean by success? What does success look like to you?" Often they reply, "Success means being rich. What should I do to make

tons of money?" And I reply, "The best way to choose a career that will make you wealthy is to not think about getting wealthy."

That may sound like double-talk, but it's sound advice, backed by scientific research. Let me explain.

In *If It Ain't Broke . . . Break It!*, Robert J. Kriegel and Louis Patler write about an extensive twenty-year study of 1,500 people who were embarking on careers in business. At the outset of the study, the researchers interviewed the participants and asked them why they chose a particular career.

The participants were divided into two groups. Group A consisted of 83 percent of the 1,500 people in the study; they had chosen their profession because they believed it would put them on the fast track to great wealth. Group B consisted of 17 percent of the participants; they had chosen their profession because they were passionate about that career and they did not worry about whether that career choice would make them wealthy.

The results are truly amazing. After twenty years, 101 of the 1,500 people in the study had become millionaires. Almost all of the millionaires—100 out of 101—came from Group B, the 17 percent group—the people who had pursued their passions instead of pursuing wealth. Only *one person* from Group A—the 83 percenters, the make-money-first group—had achieved the goal of becoming a millionaire. Those who pragmatically tried to choose a lucrative career path failed; those who followed their passion succeeded.

Filmmaker Orson Welles said, "Work is not a four-letter word. It's the thing you can get the most joy out of. . . . You just have to choose the most important thing in your life.

You must follow your heart's desire. Don't worry about the money, just *do* it because that's what God created you to do and be."[22]

If you want to be successful—including financially successful—don't chase money. Pursue your passion.

5. *Let your passion set you apart as unique.* How does your passion mark you as uniquely *you*? How does your passion make you inimitable and irreplaceable?

Now, I'm not saying that your passion *must* set you apart as unique in order to be *the* passion that propels you to success. I was certainly not the only boy to grow up dreaming of becoming a professional baseball player, nor was I the only adult who has had a passion for sports management or public speaking or writing. But if you do happen to have a burning desire in you to accomplish something that no one else is attempting, to solve a problem that no one else is working on, to meet a need that the rest of the world is ignoring—*pay attention to that unique passion.* The very uniqueness of your passion might be the very factor that makes the whole world sit up and take notice.

Chris Guillebeau is an American entrepreneur and author, best known for *The Art of Non-Conformity*. He observes:

> *You need passion.* You need to be absolutely passionate about what you believe in. If you don't feel passionate about anything, chances are you haven't discovered what you're really good at yet. Keep looking.
>
> *You need a vision and a task.* The vision tells you where you are going; the task tells you what to do next to get there.
>
> *You need the answers to the two most important questions in the universe.* What do you really want to get out of life?

> How can you help others in a way that no one else can? Once you have the answers, you'll be ahead of most everyone else.[23]

Take special note of that second question: How can you help others *in a way that no one else can*? In other words, how does your own heartfelt, personal, individual passion make you special and irreplaceable to others? What do you offer to your employers, your customers, your clients, your students, your readers, your listeners, your constituents that no one else offers? A lot of people have the same natural talents you have. A lot of people have the same education you have, the same background you have, the same principles and beliefs you have.

If you are going to offer the world something no one else offers, your best bet is to offer a unique passion—something you care about in a way and to a degree that no one else does. If you have an overwhelming, obsessive passion that drives you and sets you apart as a one-in-a-million individual, you are well on your way to achieving your dreams of success.

Michael Jordan had a unique passion for being the best basketball player on earth. Nelson Mandela had a unique passion for racial justice in South Africa. Dr. Billy Graham has a unique passion for serving God and winning souls. Mahatma Gandhi had a unique passion for human rights and Indian independence. Evel Knievel had a unique passion for performing death-defying stunts on motorcycles.

Dr. Martin Luther King Jr. had a uniquely passionate dream of equality, justice, and racial harmony. Dr. Jonas Salk had a unique passion to conquer polio. Robert Goddard had a unique passion for rocketry. Pope John Paul II had a unique passion for global peace, justice, and forgiveness. Ronald Reagan had a unique passion for collapsing the Soviet "evil empire."

King Solomon had a unique passion for wisdom. Muhammad Ali had a unique passion for being The Greatest. Cesar Chavez had a unique passion for lifting farm laborers out of poverty. Jesse Owens had a unique passion for Olympic competition. Mother Teresa had a unique passion for service to God's holy poor.

These individuals are remembered for their unique contributions to history or religion or civil rights or science or sports. Each was a one-of-a-kind individual. They marked history with the force of their unique passions.

And you can make your mark, wherever you are, whatever you do, if you have a unique and irreplaceable passion. Thomas Friedman, Pulitzer-winning columnist for the *New York Times*, offers this advice:

> Do what you love. This is not sappy career advice but an absolute survival strategy, because, as I like to put it, the world is getting flat. What is flattening the world is our ability to automate more work with computers and software and to transmit that work anywhere in the world so that it can be done more efficiently or cheaply. . . . The flatter the world gets, the more essential it is that you do what you love, because all the boring, repetitive jobs are going to be automated or outsourced in a flat world. The good jobs that will remain are those that cannot be automated or outsourced; they are the jobs that demand or encourage some uniquely human creative flair, passion, and imagination. In other words, jobs that can be done only by people who love what they do.[24]

When Friedman says "people who love what they do," he is talking about people who are intensely passionate—so passionate for their work and their beliefs that they cannot be replaced or even compared to anyone else. Make your overriding passion your brand, your mark of distinction. Own it—and become uniquely, irreplaceably *you*.

6. *Use passion to fuel your practice and preparation.* Some people love to practice and prepare, and others absolutely hate it. Whether you love to practice or you hate it, your passion can fuel you and motivate you to put forth your ultimate effort.

Super Bowl–winning quarterback Peyton Manning is one of those freaks of nature who just loves a hard, grueling practice session. "For me," he once said, "it's not just about the game. I mean I love practice. A lot of guys don't. I like going to practice."[25] That's passion talking—passion for the game, passion for winning, passion for being the best.

You may think, *That's fine for Peyton Manning—but what about us mere mortals who hate to work out and train and suffer through a tough practice? What if I don't have a natural passion for practice and preparation?*

That's okay. Some of the highest-achieving performers in the world hated to practice. But they practiced anyway, because they had a passion that carried them through the suffering, pain, and sheer exhaustion that comes with intense practice and preparation. One of those was the greatest boxer of all time, Muhammad Ali. He was once asked if he enjoyed training for big boxing matches. The Champ replied, "I hated every minute of training, but I said to myself, 'Don't quit, suffer now, and live the rest of your life as a champion.'"[26]

Whether you love to train like Peyton Manning or hate to train like Muhammad Ali, passion will get you through it, passion will motivate you to persevere, passion will enable you to push beyond the limits of your endurance. If you don't have a passion for preparation, ask yourself, "What *do* I have a passion for?" If you really want to succeed, you can summon a passion from within, a passion that will motivate you through the tough times and grueling training sessions.

Bestselling author Jentezen Franklin told me something I'll never forget when he was a guest on my Orlando radio show: "When you discover your passion in life and pursue it relentlessly, you become like a heat-seeking missile." A heat-seeking missile searches for a source of heat, locks onto it, then chases it with a single-minded focus. If the heat source moves right, the missile veers right. If the heat source soars, dives, or zigzags, the missile relentlessly pursues. In the same way, your focused passion enables you to unerringly track even a moving target of success.

In *Telling Lies for Fun and Profit*, novelist Lawrence Block tells the story of a young musician who approached a world-renowned violinist for encouragement. "Master," the young man said, "I want to pursue a career in music. I know I play well, but I don't know if I have the talent for true greatness. I don't want to waste my life if I don't have a truly great talent. But let me play for you, and if you encourage me to go on, then I will devote my life to music."

The master violinist said, "Play."

The young man raised his violin and bow, then poured out his heart and soul through his instrument. He played with feeling, he played flawlessly, and when he had finished playing, he knew he had delivered the best performance of his life. He waited for the verdict.

The master shook his head. “You lack the fire,” he said.

The young violinist was devastated. His greatest performance was condemned by the master. He turned and walked away in despair.

Years went by. In all those years, the would-be violinist never played another note. Instead, he pursued a career in business, and became quite prosperous. One day, he heard that the master violinist was giving a performance in town, so he went to the hotel to call upon the great violinist. He knocked on the hotel room door. The old violinist appeared at the door. “Yes?”

“Years ago, I played my violin for you.”

“Oh? Well, I meet so many young musicians.”

“You changed my life. I was ready to devote myself to a career in music, but you told me I lacked the fire. So I chose a career in business instead. I’ve done well, I’ve had a good life, but I’ve always wondered—how could you tell from just one performance that I lacked the fire?”

“I didn’t pay any attention when you played,” the master said. “Whenever a young violinist plays for me, I always say, ‘You lack the fire.’”

The businessman stared at the master in astonishment and rage. “How could you do that to me? I could have been a great violinist—all I needed was one word of encouragement from you. But you dashed my hopes and I believed you. That’s unforgivable.”

The master was unmoved. “I said you lacked the fire, and I was right. If you’d had the fire to be a great musician, no words of mine would have mattered. Nothing would have kept you from your dream—if you had the fire.”[27]

The fire the master spoke of is a thing called *passion*. If you live your life with passion, every day will be filled with wonder and significance. Your focused passion will enable you to work harder, persevere through obstacles, and achieve the impossible.

Novelist E. M. Forster is quoted as saying, “One person with passion is better than forty people merely interested.” Don’t be content to live in the gray areas of life. Ignite the fire within you. Focus your passion.

6

Energized with Confidence

> What goals would you be setting for yourself if you knew you could not fail?
>
> **ROBERT H. SCHULLER**, minister and author

THE WORLD IS FULL of dream-stompers and confidence-killers. Everyone who tries to accomplish anything worthwhile will inevitably encounter opposition, scorn, and ridicule. For example, I recently heard about a brutal one-star reader review of a book sold on Amazon.com. Here (spelling and grammatical errors and all) is the review:

> This is possibly the worst book ever written.
>
> In fact, it is the worst material ever made. This story is so depressingly bad, it made me weep after wards at how badly I had wasted my time. My back had already been aching

> from having to pick the book out of the lowest book shelf, and my hand was shaking from the effort of having to turn around the pages.
>
> And then came the story. I wanted so badly to run away screaming, but the shock had taken the breath out of me, and my feet had fallen asleep from this dreadful story. It had no virtue, no truth, no reason, no sense, no NOTHING!
>
> I wanted to destroy the memory of it any way possible. But there will be no turning back from this. This is why children cry; why dogs lick themselves; why the rivers run downhill instead of uphill. Oh, oh, the effort just to write this warning! Please, take heed, don't waste time and money for this book!!![1]

What is the book this reviewer calls "possibly the worst book ever written"? *Harry Potter and the Sorcerer's Stone* by J. K. Rowling—one of the bestselling books in the history of publishing, with well over a hundred million copies in print. Dream-stompers are out there, and they go after everybody, even the creator of Harry Potter.

Bruce Williams hosted a nationally syndicated call-in talk show for twenty-nine years, from 1981 to 2010. I once heard a story he told about an encounter with a professor during his college days. Bruce was a sophomore in his midtwenties, married with two children, employed by the school to run the school snack bar for the princely sum of eighty bucks a week.

"My boss, the professor," Bruce said, "had once run a snack bar in a drive-in theater. One day I said, 'Professor, it's pretty tough going through school and feeding a wife and two kids on eighty bucks a week. I need a twenty-dollar raise.' The professor said, 'Williams, you have grandiose ideas. You'll never be worth a hundred dollars a week.'"

Time passed, and Bruce Williams became a successful businessman, was elected mayor of Franklin Township, New Jersey (two terms), and became a successful radio personality. The school where young Bruce Williams had once run the snack bar invited him to sit on the board of trustees. Bruce declined the invitation, but he did return to the campus to meet with the board and thank them for the invitation.

Over the years, whenever he faced obstacles or opposition and he was tempted to quit, he'd hear his old professor's words spurring him on: "Williams, you have grandiose ideas." That professor actually helped to inspire Bruce's success.

"Someday," Bruce Williams concluded, "I may go back and pay the professor a visit. But if I do, it'll be to thank him for telling me I had grandiose ideas."

Beware the Dream Stompers and Confidence Killers

We all have dreams, passions, and talents. Yet all too many of us live our lives without ever achieving our dreams or realizing the full potential of our passions and talents. Why is that? Why do so many people settle for lives of averageness when a lifetime of success is within their grasp?

I believe many of us settle for mediocrity because we lack the confidence to pursue our passions. We have all the talent we need to succeed. And we started out with a passionate vision of future success. But somewhere along the way, something happened that shook our confidence and stifled our passion. So we have set our passion on a shelf and placed our talent in a drawer, and there they sit, unused and unfulfilled.

Some people have fallen for the myth that success is a matter of luck, like winning the lottery. But successful people didn't just "luck into" success—they made careful plans, they made the right decisions, they took the right actions, they worked hard and took risks, they persevered through obstacles and opposition, they ignored the criticism and ridicule of the dream-stompers, and they prevailed.

Don't waste your life waiting for your "luck" to change. Don't think about luck at all. Successful people don't wait for opportunities to come knocking. They summon their talent, passion, and confidence, and then they pick up a battering ram and charge through the door, never looking back.

In addition to the human dream-stompers that stand in our way, we all face internal confidence-killers that seek to smother our passion and keep us from our dreams. These internal saboteurs include aversion to risk and resistance to change.

1. *Aversion to risk*. Most people are overly security conscious. They think, "I want to be successful, but I don't want to take the risks that lead to success. I don't want to put my time, my money, or my reputation at risk. What if I take a risk—and I fail?"

The moment you decide to avoid risk, the moment you decide to play it safe, you might as well toss your goals and dreams in the dumpster. No one ever achieved anything worthwhile without taking risks. If you aren't willing to risk your time, your resources, your comfort, and your reputation, then let's face it, you've surrendered your dreams without a fight.

Producer and talent manager Ken Kragen was the force behind the song "We Are the World." He once said, "If you want to achieve great things in life, you have to take risks. The first risk is daring to feel deeply, to be passionate about what you want and care about. Enthusiasm is the key to breaking through barriers, whether your dream is to touch one person or millions."[2]

Everybody experiences fear. Successful people have learned to manage and overcome their fears. Everyone knows the experience of wondering, "What if I fail? What if I fall flat on my face? What if I lose everything?" Successful people have asked all those same questions—but they tell themselves, "If I don't try, I'll fail as badly as if I had tried and lost. So I might as well make the attempt and give it everything I've got."

We can talk ourselves into all kinds of reasons for not chasing our dreams with a passion—but it all boils down to being paralyzed by fear. Don't spend the rest of your life living in a twilight of regret. Don't spend the rest of your life wondering what you might have achieved if only you had dared. Don't surrender to the confidence-killer. Summon your courage. Dare to succeed.

2. *Resistance to change.* Some people are actually afraid of success. Why? Because if they succeed, their lives will be changed. There's something about the human psyche that resists change—even exciting, exhilarating, positive change. There is something within us that wants to maintain the familiar, the status quo, even when the status quo is miserable.

For some people, the very thought of change—even the change that comes with success—makes them anxious and apprehensive. They wonder, "What if I can't handle success? What if I can't handle the attention and responsibility that come with success? What if I have to give up my privacy and my quiet, simple lifestyle?" Change is stressful and it stirs up the fear of the unknown, and that's why many people are afraid of success.

Aversion to risk and resistance to change are two confidence-killers that can block our path to success—but only if we surrender to them. The good news is that we can conquer these confidence-killers. And once we have vanquished them, we are free to pursue our passion and talent all the way to the fulfillment of our dreams.

Edna Staebler was born in Kitchener, Ontario, and spent much of her early life reading books she lugged home from the public library. "Nothing exciting happened to me," she later recalled. "Kitchener and my dates seemed very dull." She attended the University of Toronto, and she told all her friends she was going to be a writer. After college, she applied for a job writing news stories for Kitchener's daily newspaper, but once she was hired, her boss assigned her to collect money from newsboys. She wasn't good at keeping track of money, so the job didn't last long.

Afraid of taking risks, afraid of failure, afraid of change, she lacked the passion and confidence to go after her dreams. She admired writers like Virginia Woolf and Mary Webb, and wanted to be like them—but instead of writing, she recalled, "I just woozled around, not knowing what to write about." She married a man who turned out to be a troubled alcoholic. He mocked her dreams of becoming a writer, and her home life turned steadily worse and worse.

One summer, eager for a vacation from her unpleasant home life, Edna Staebler traveled to Nova Scotia to visit her sister for a few days. She ended up spending two weeks in a tiny fishing village, Neil's Harbour. Every day, she told herself she needed to return home—yet she found it impossible to leave. Never before had she felt so alive.

One day, she went out on the sea with the fishermen of Neil's Harbour. Another day, she square-danced at the Orange Lodge Hall. She grew to know and love the men, women, and children of the village. One morning, she awoke and said to herself, "That's it! I'll write about Neil's Harbour!"

Returning to her home in Kitchener, Staebler wrote down all her memories of the fishing village—the voices of the people, the sound and emotions of the sea, the colors of the land and sky. Finally, she felt she had found herself as a writer. She wrote with passion and enthusiasm, filling pages and pages of notebooks with stories and dialogue and vivid impressions.

And that is when her dream-stomper struck—and this time it was her own mother. While Staebler was in the midst of writing her stories, her mother came to visit and found her hard at work. "Why waste your time, Edna?" her mother said. "You can't be a writer. You have to have talent to be a writer."

Instantly, Edna Staebler's confidence wilted, and her passion for writing was shattered into a million pieces. Her imagination froze. Her memories stopped flowing. Thanks to her mother's cruel words, she had just discovered the terrifying experience known as writer's block.

A few days later, a noted author came to Kitchener to speak to the local women's club. Dispirited and discouraged by her mother's words, Edna Staebler attended the author's talk. After his presentation, she went up to him and showed him some of her stories in her notebooks. She was terrified of what he would say, and expected this published author to condemn her work, just as her husband and mother had.

"This is good work," the author told her. "I mean it. You must keep writing and submit your work for publication." Even after the author left town, he continued to send her notes of encouragement, telling her to keep writing and to believe in herself.

Finally, she selected one of her stories about Neil's Harbour and submitted it to the Canadian magazine *Maclean's*. To her amazement, it was immediately accepted—her first-ever submission was her first sale. She was fifty years old when she made that sale—it had taken her that long to realize her childhood dream of becoming a writer.

Not long after she made that sale, her husband ran off with her best friend, leaving her alone to support herself. She decided it was time to take a risk and try to build a career as a writer. She established a regular working schedule, and writing became her day job. She produced scores of articles, submitted them for publication, and her work began appearing regularly in *Maclean's*, *Chatelaine*, *Saturday Night*, *Reader's Digest*, and other magazines.

She published her first book at age sixty. Her most important book, *Cape Breton Harbour*, based on her two weeks in the fishing village, was released when she was sixty-six. She died in 2006 at age one hundred, fifty years after making her first professional sale. Her writing career began at the exact midpoint of her life—and it happened when she stopped listening to her fears, stopped listening to the dream-stompers in her life, and finally summoned the confidence to achieve her dreams.[3]

As another writer, Diane Ackerman, once observed, "The best advice on writing I ever received was: Invent your confidence. When you're trying something new, insecurity and stage fright come with the territory. . . . How could it be otherwise? By its nature, art involves risk."[4]

A Lifetime of Passion—or a Lifetime of Regret?

Former NBA star Bill Bradley served three terms as a United States senator from New Jersey. I once heard him tell a story about a conversation he had at a postgame reception in Chicago in the 1970s. A man approached him and asked, "Do you really like to play basketball?"

"Absolutely," Bradley said. "I love basketball more than anything else I could be doing right now."

"That's great. I think I know how that feels—to really love something you're doing. I used to play the trumpet, and that's how I felt about performing. I played in a band, and we performed on college campuses. We were good. A record company offered us a contract to record and tour. The rest of the band wanted to sign the contract, but I decided not to."

"Oh? Why didn't you go for it?"

"My dad told me I shouldn't do it. He said there's no security in a music career."

"Did you agree with your father?"

"I guess so. I mean, it's true that it's not a secure way to live—a life on the road, performing here and there, no steady income. My dad suggested a career as a lawyer. So I went to law school and now I'm a lawyer."

"Do you ever play the trumpet?"

"Every once in a while. Not much. I don't have time anymore."

"Do you like the law?"

"It's okay, I guess. But nothing like playing the trumpet."

Now, there's nothing wrong with a career as a lawyer—especially if you have a passion for justice. But if you have a passion for the trumpet, and you default to becoming a lawyer just because it seems more secure, you may be short-changing yourself—and you may spend the rest of your life living with your regrets. Instead of wondering what might have been, why not follow your passion, apply your talent, and see where it takes you?

Thanks to my mother's passion for civil rights, I was on the National Mall in Washington DC, along with my mother and sister, on August 28, 1963—the day Dr. Martin Luther King Jr., gave his "I Have a Dream" speech. I was a witness to history when Dr. King spoke with such eloquence and passion about his dream for racial harmony in America. He could have easily chosen to live his life out of the limelight, preaching safe sermons week after week at the Dexter Avenue Baptist Church in Montgomery, Alabama—but his dream was too powerful, his passion too strong, so he took the battle for civil rights to a national stage. Even after he was slain by an assassin's bullet, his dream and his passion lived on and changed the soul of America.

In order to defeat the dream-stompers without and the confidence-killers within, you must become what I call a "practical dreamer," someone who knows how to dream big dreams, then finds the practical steps to turn those dreams into reality. One of the most accomplished practical dreamers I know is my wife, Ruth. She is a time management consultant for Franklin Covey, a life coach, an author, a mother, a marathon runner, and my inspiration. She makes her living teaching people how to dream their dreams—then live them. She says there are four questions all practical dreamers must ask themselves in order to transform dreams into reality:

1. "*Why do I want to achieve this dream?*" Why am I passionate about this particular dream? How is this dream connected to my values, my purpose for living, my faith, my calling, my family, and my goals? This is the first question we have to ask ourselves, because it is foundational. In order to have the passion and motivation to see our dreams and goals through to completion, our dream must be deeply connected to our most cherished values, beliefs, and desires.

2. "*When do I want to achieve my dream?*" It's important to know not only where we want to be, but when we want to get there. A dream without a deadline is just a daydream. Deadlines motivate us to work harder, work longer, and set priorities in order to reach our goals.

3. "*What are the specific steps I must take to achieve this dream?*" The practical steps we must take in order to achieve our goals must be clearly defined and measurable. At each step along the way, we should be able to point to certain benchmarks and say, "Here's where I am in my journey. I've come this far, and I have this far to go to reach my destination." This tells us if we are on track, ahead of schedule, or running behind. If we can't accurately measure our progress, how will we know when we reach our destination?

4. "*What steps must I take today in order to reach my goals tomorrow?*" It's fine to have big goals and extreme dreams for the future. But we will never achieve those goals

and dreams unless we are taking daily steps that lead us to our destination. It helps to take our big, audacious goals and break them down into a series of intermediate tasks and deadlines. Most of us will achieve success not in a single Superman-sized leap, but in a series of baby steps. At the beginning of each day, you look at your "Things to Do" list and say, "These are the baby steps I need to take today in order to achieve my goal."

Ask yourself these four questions on a regular basis, and you will make sure that you are a practical dreamer, not a daydreamer. These four questions will enable you to take responsibility for your extreme dreams, so you can make those dreams come true.

Practical dreamers have shaped our history and produced all of the achievements that we now take for granted: the founding of America, the civil rights movement, the inventions of Thomas Edison, great works of literature like the plays of Shakespeare and the novels of Charles Dickens and John Steinbeck, the first polio vaccine, the carved monument on Mount Rushmore, the Apollo missions to the moon, and so much more. Each of these achievements began with a dream, and each was transformed into reality by practical dreamers. Today we live out the dreams of men and women who dared to take risks, conquer fear, and become agents of change.

I hope you will be inspired to become a practical dreamer and join their ranks. I hope you will take some risks, conquer your fears, and change the world. Live a lifetime of passion, amplified by your talent, and energized by your confidence—not a lifetime of regret.

Energized with Confidence

Farrah Gray started his first business at age six. Growing up poor on Chicago's South Side, he dreamed of making money and escaping poverty. His first business involved painting rocks and turning them into such products as bookends and paperweights. He made a fifty dollar profit on the venture, and later reflected, "There's no idea dumb enough that you can't get at least a billion people to buy into it."

The young entrepreneur went on to launch a brand of body lotions and a line of prepaid phone cards, and by age fifteen, he was a millionaire. He hosted his own radio talk show, "Youth AM/FM." Before his twentieth birthday, he published the first of several books, *Reallionaire: Nine Steps to Becoming Rich from the Inside Out*. In that book, he observed:

> I've learned that true success isn't so much about being talented as it is about what you do with that talent. . . . It's about how we recognize and actualize our unique gifts. That's what will take us to that next level of achievement and abundance. For me, that's when you become a "reallionaire"—someone who pursues his or her passion with authenticity, sincerity, and honesty.[5]

What was the key to turning Farrah Gray's dreams into money-making realities? *The intersection of his talent for selling and his passion for success.* From his boyhood, Farrah Gray has understood that talent alone is not enough. His natural selling abilities needed to be "actualized" by his authentic passion. That was his success intersection.

Whatever you set out to accomplish, you must passionately want it, and you must confidently believe you can achieve it, or you'll never get started. "To succeed," Farrah Gray says, "entrepreneurs have to believe in themselves and in their ability to achieve the goals they have set for themselves. This is often shown by a belief that 'if you want something badly enough and are prepared to work at it, you'll usually get it.'"[6]

Margaret Thatcher was prime minister of Great Britain from 1979 to 1990, and she was one of the greatest examples of self-confidence the world has ever seen. She believed in herself without being arrogant, and she asserted herself without being abrasive. She demonstrated a confident attitude from an early age. When she was nine, young Margaret received a prize for excellent schoolwork. When someone told her she was lucky to have received the prize, she said, "I wasn't lucky. I deserved it."

She earned a degree in chemistry at Oxford, and though she would later gain fame as the first woman prime minister, she was actually more proud of being the first prime minister with a degree in science. In 1948, she was rejected for a job at Imperial Chemical Industries because (as the note in her application file stated), "This woman is headstrong, obstinate and dangerously self-opinionated." In other words, she had the makings of a leader.

In January 1976, when Mrs. Thatcher was a member of Parliament and the leader of the opposition, she delivered a speech, "Britain Awake," at Kensington Town Hall. Her speech, a blistering condemnation of Soviet expansionism, made headlines around the world. She said:

> The men in the Soviet politburo don't have to worry about the ebb and flow of public opinion. They put guns before butter, while we put just about everything before guns.

> They know that they are a super power in only one sense—the military sense. They are a failure in human and economic terms.
>
> But let us make no mistake. The Russians calculate that their military strength will more than make up for their economic and social weakness. They are determined to use it in order to get what they want from us.[7]

Mrs. Thatcher's remarks sent shockwaves around the world. She made this speech during the era of détente, when Western politicians walked on eggshells around the Soviets. This was seven years before Ronald Reagan's controversial "Evil Empire" speech in 1983. At that time, bluntly calling the Soviets out for their military expansionism simply was not done.

The Soviets were livid, and the Soviet Defense Ministry newspaper *Krasnaya Zvezda* (Red Star) mockingly called her "the Iron Lady." Mrs. Thatcher took the intended insult as a compliment. The display of Soviet outrage only increased Mrs. Thatcher's stature in Great Britain. Soon people throughout Great Britain and around the world called her "the Iron Lady."

In 1978, the former governor of California, Ronald Reagan, visited Mrs. Thatcher, and they had a long conversation over tea. During their conversation, Reagan told Mrs. Thatcher that he "intended to try and become president." In reply, Margaret Thatcher confidently predicted, "I *am* going to become prime minister." Reagan liked her style. In 1979, Mrs. Thatcher achieved her goal, and in 1981, Reagan achieved his. The two world leaders became close friends and worked together to engineer the collapse of Soviet communism.

Soon after taking office as prime minister, Mrs. Thatcher introduced a slate of free-market economic initiatives that emphasized lower taxes, deregulation, and spending restraint. During her first two years in office, the economy remained sluggish—and her popularity began to slip. By the fall of 1980, her critics in the media and the opposing party demanded that she make a U-turn and reverse her economic policies. Supremely confident that her policies would soon take hold and restore prosperity, she gave a speech declaring, "To those waiting with bated breath for that favorite media catchphrase, the U-turn, I have only one thing to say: You turn if you want to. The lady's not for turning."

By the time she stood for reelection in 1983, the economy had rebounded and she won easily. And she won again in 1987. Her confidence in her economic policies was vindicated, and a grateful nation made her the longest-serving British prime minister of the twentieth century.

In the summer of 1990, when Iraq under Saddam Hussein invaded its tiny neighbor, Kuwait, Mrs. Thatcher was in the United States meeting with President George H. W. Bush and other leaders at a conference in Aspen, Colorado. Upon hearing of the invasion, she went to the home where President Bush was staying and told him, "Aggressors must be stopped, and not only stopped, but they must be thrown out. An aggressor cannot gain from his aggression."

President Bush, however, was receiving conflicting advice from his cabinet and from other world leaders. Margaret Thatcher was alarmed that the American president seemed indecisive at a time when bold, confident action was needed. "Look, George," she said, "this is no time to go wobbly."

The confidence of "the Iron Lady" persuaded President Bush to commit American forces to the region. Her confident words changed the mind of the American president—and changed the course of world events.

On two occasions, I attended events in Orlando where Mrs. Thatcher was the keynote speaker. I was captivated by her passion, her wit, and her stories about great people and great events. Most of all, I was impressed by her confidence as a leader. When she told her opponents, "The lady's not for turning," she silenced them with her absolute confidence. And when she told George H. W. Bush "this is no time to go wobbly," she transplanted her confidence into the heart of the American president.

Great leaders are not for turning, and they must not go wobbly. To achieve your goals, you need the confidence of your passion and your convictions. When you demonstrate to everyone around that *you* believe in *you*, they will believe in you as well.

Where Does Confidence Come From?

The secret of success is the intersection of your talent and your passion. When your greatest talent intersects with your strongest passion, you've discovered your sweet spot in life. But in order to pursue your passion, you must have confidence in your talent. Where does that confidence come from?

1. *Confidence comes from doing.* Michael Jordan was known as the player you can trust with the clutch shot. When everything was on the line, you knew that Jordan wouldn't choke. He would confidently make the game-winning shot.

Jordan recalls that he learned to be confident in clutch situations during the 1982 NCAA Championship Game between the Georgetown Hoyas and the North Carolina Tar Heels.

With just over a minute remaining, Georgetown scored to take the lead, 62–61. During the time-out, North Carolina coach Dean Smith told Michael and his teammates that Georgetown would focus on heavily guarding forward James Worthy and center Sam Perkins, leaving young guard Michael Jordan wide open. "We're going to try to get the ball in to James," Smith said. "But James, if you can't get it up, swing it around. Michael should have a wide-open shot."

Jordan recalls, "The play was designed for James Worthy, not me. . . . I knew I was the second option, so it wasn't as if the weight was on me."

The ball was inbounded and North Carolina worked it around, trying to get the ball to an open man. Point guard Jimmy Black passed to Jordan on the left wing, and Jordan drained the jump shot with 17 seconds remaining. "By the time the ball got to me," Jordan said, "I just had to react."

Georgetown was unable to answer back, and North Carolina won, 63–62.

"If we'd had a different play set up," Jordan said, "or if I'd thought about it in the time-out? I don't know, maybe things would have turned out different. . . . At really clutch times, some people try to con themselves into thinking none of it matters. But I also know that's just a rationalization, because it does matter."

Michael Jordan traces his confidence in the clutch to that one shot in the championship game. "My whole NBA career I always thought back on 1982. I'm not saying you can't be confident in the clutch if you've never made the big play before—obviously, I was already confident before that shot. But that one moment initiated so much. Every shot after that, I felt I could make. I responded so well in those situations because I had such positive thoughts. I thrived on last-second shots. It became a trait for me."[8]

Pete Carroll has been head football coach of the USC Trojans, the New England Patriots, and the New York Jets. He is currently head football coach and executive vice president of the Seattle Seahawks. In his book *Win Forever*, Carroll tells how he learned confidence from one of his sports heroes. He was fifteen years old, reading a magazine story about NBA Hall of Famer Rick Barry. During the interview, Barry was shooting jump shots from the top of the key—and he was making every shot. Pete Carroll recalls the conversation:

> "Hey, Rick," the reporter asked. "Do you have a philosophy of life, or some principle that guides you?" Rick turned to him, with an arrogant look that was practically a trademark, and simply said, "Yeah—I'm a 46 percent lifetime shooter. If I miss my first ten shots, look out!" . . .
>
> I was struck by that statement and by what an extraordinary illustration of self-confidence it was. Rick was then only five years, give or take, into his fourteen-year NBA/ABA career. Just think about how well he must have known himself back then to espouse such an all-encompassing philosophy. He was saying, *I know myself so well that if I miss my first ten shots, you had better look out because I know I'm going to make my next ten . . . . give or take a few.* That wasn't a prediction, it was a statement of fact. . . .
>
> Certainty like that comes not merely from a high estimation of one's own talent, but from a deep knowledge of one's strengths and weaknesses. This principle has become

one of the pillars of my philosophy both personally and professionally.[9]

The more you exercise your talent, the better you get to know your talent—your strengths and weaknesses—and the more confidence you have. Not only did Rick Barry gain confidence by doing, but he taught a teenage athlete how to build his own confidence through doing—and that early lesson in confidence helped Pete Carroll become one of the elite coaches in both college and NFL football.

Duke University basketball coach Mike Krzyzewski put it this way: "With accomplishments comes confidence and with confidence comes belief. It has to be in that order."[10]

Confidence comes from doing. Every time you overcome a challenge, every time you conquer a fear, every time you take a risk and succeed, you ratchet your confidence up another notch. Don't wait for your confidence to come find you. Go out and seize your confidence by doing the thing that scares you. Every success you experience is another rung on the ladder to your ultimate goal.

2. *Confidence comes from preparation.* Don't take my word for it—take the word of NBA Hall of Famer John Havlicek: "Confidence comes from preparation and the only way to be fully prepared is to practice something until you have it down so well that you know it will work."[11]

Boston Celtics legend Larry Bird agrees. "I lose confidence when I'm not practicing," Bird once said. "When I was out there and I hadn't practiced, I didn't have the same feeling. It was like going in to take a test and you didn't study, and you don't know what's on the test. When you study and you know what's on there, it's a breeze to go through it."[12]

Jackie MacMullan, NBA columnist for ESPN.com, describes how Larry Bird displayed his confidence during the 1986 All-Star weekend. That was the year the NBA instituted the three-point contest at the All-Star festivities—a chance for the top long-range shooters in the league to showcase their talent. MacMullan writes:

> On the day of the competition, Boston Celtics forward Larry Bird sauntered into the locker room where his fellow participants were dressing.
>
> "Hey, guys," Bird chortled. "Which one of you is going to finish second?"
>
> It's one thing to say it. It's another thing to back it up. Bird validated his bravado by easily outdistancing Craig Hodges 22–12 in the finals—even though he had finished fourth in the preliminary round and just barely advanced. But as the field narrowed, Bird's shooting improved. The higher the stakes, the more confident he became. . . .
>
> "At that point of my career, I had all the confidence in the world," Bird said. "When I took a shot, I believed it was going in, every time. I had taken so many shots, I couldn't imagine missing. I only thought in positive terms.[13]

When you invest in your preparation, you invest in your confidence and your talent.

3. *Confidence is a choice.* When you are struggling to build your confidence, you may find it hard to believe, but it's absolutely true: *you can choose to be confident in any situation.* Entrepreneur and author Seth Godin put it this way:

> Effective confidence comes from within, it's not the result of external events. The confident salesperson is likely to close more sales. The confident violinist expresses more of the music. The confident leader points us to the places we want (and need) to go.
>
> You succeed because you've chosen to be confident. It's not really useful to require yourself to be successful before you're able to become confident.[14]

Peanuts creator Charles Shultz is quoted as saying, "Life is a ten-speed bike. Most of us have gears we never use." Many of us have talent and passion, but we limit ourselves by our lack of confidence. When we don't feel confident, we need to "bootstrap" our confidence. We have to summon the confidence and bravado that we don't actually feel.

If you think you can't win the election, run anyway. If you think you can't write that novel, start writing anyway. If you think you can't learn to play funky jazz saxophone, pick up an E-flat alto sax, take some lessons, and prove yourself wrong. If you choose to have the confidence to begin, the confidence to succeed will probably come. Whenever you think you can't do something, tell yourself, "I *can* do this." Ask yourself, "Why not me?" Then *do* it.

Hungarian psychiatrist Thomas S. Szasz once observed, "Clear thinking requires courage rather than intelligence."[15] It's true. We can create confidence out of sheer courage—and confidence will give us a clear-eyed perspective on the challenges we face. Confidence enables us to focus more intensely and perform more effectively. When we choose to act on our courage and our confidence instead of shrinking back in fear, we are better able to solve problems and increase the odds of a positive outcome.

Confident people are not paralyzed by fear. They are energized by courage and passion. They trust their instincts and listen to their intuition. They make high-quality decisions, under pressure and in real time, and they achieve their goals.

As my friend Rich DeVos, co-owner of the Orlando Magic, once wrote, "We choose to be confident. We choose to believe in ourselves and our goals. Confidence is both a choice and a gift. If you didn't receive the gift, you can make the choice. When you make the choice, you receive the gift. . . . Confidence will come in the doing."[16]

Trust your God-given talent. Ignite your God-given passion. Then energize your confidence and *soar*.

7

Multiply Your Success

THE POWER OF TEAMWORK

> Teamwork is the beauty of our sport, where you have five acting as one. You become selfless.
>
> **MIKE KRZYZEWSKI**, basketball coach

On Friday, January 7, 2011, I spent the entire day, from 7:00 a.m. to 5:00 p.m., undergoing intensive testing at Florida Hospital's Celebration Health Assessment Center. At the end of testing, Dr. Christine Edwards said, "Pat, everything looks good, except there's something in your blood work we're not sure about. You ought to have it checked by your primary physician."

I didn't know it then, but that little anomaly in my blood work was about to turn my world upside-down.

Two days later, I ran in the Walt Disney World Marathon—my fifty-eighth marathon. At age seventy, I had been running marathons for fifteen years. Afterward I felt fine. Nothing but the usual soreness.

Three days after the marathon, I woke up writhing in pain, with agony radiating from my spine. I couldn't move. I couldn't get out of bed. I had never experienced such pain. After extensive x-rays and an MRI, a back specialist could find no reason for my pain.

On January 13, I went to my primary care physician, Dr. Vince Wilson. After examining the report on my blood work from Celebration Health Assessment Center, he looked troubled—and his first words alarmed me: "Why do things happen to all the good people?"

"What do you mean, Doc?"

"There's something in your blood work, Pat—an abnormal protein called a paraprotein. I hope I'm wrong, but I have a suspicion. I'm going to refer you to one of the best experts in the field, Dr. Robert Reynolds."

I didn't know until I arrived at Dr. Reynolds's office that he was an oncologist and hematologist—a specialist in cancer and diseases of the blood. Dr. Reynolds told me, "Pat, it appears you have multiple myeloma—cancer of the plasma cells in the blood and bone marrow."

Instantly, my denial kicked into high gear. Yes, I'd heard him say "cancer"—but he also said "it appears." The blood test could be wrong. I might not have the "C word" after all.

Dr. Reynolds ordered extensive tests. I told myself that once the tests were completed, he'd say, "Sorry we gave you a scare, Pat—turns out it wasn't cancer after all."

I told myself there was no reason to worry my wife, since it was all a false alarm. But as the day of my next appointment approached, I decided I wanted Ruth to come with me—just in case. She was baffled by my request but agreed to go. On the way to the appointment, she looked at the letter I had received from Dr. Reynolds—and she gasped. "Pat," she said, "he's an *oncologist*. You didn't tell me this is cancer!"

"Oh, it's nothing like that. They just found something unusual in my blood."

But when we sat down to discuss the test findings, Dr. Reynolds told me, straight from the shoulder, "It's cancer, Pat. You have multiple myeloma."

From a state of denial, I went straight to despair. I thought it was a death sentence. Dr. Reynolds handed me a tissue, and I mopped my eyes while mentally planning my own funeral.

Instantly, Ruth took over and began asking important, practical questions, and she took notes on all of Dr. Reynolds's answers. Dr. Reynolds told me I had good reason for hope. He said I had a 70 to 75 percent chance of remission with chemotherapy. And he said that, because of extensive research, myeloma patients are living longer than ever before.

"Pat," he said, "multiple myeloma isn't curable, but it's very treatable. Our goal is remission. I honestly think you're going to do well with this."

Before I left Dr. Reynolds's office, I was struck by an inspiration: "Doc, how about this for a motivational slogan? 'The Mission Is Remission.'"

"I like it," he said. "We'll start chemotherapy immediately and move as aggressively as we can."

"I'm in your hands, Doc. Let's get going."

For the better part of the year, my medical team pumped an assortment of drugs into me, trying to bring my numbers down. It soon became clear that the treatments weren't working. I learned that what we call multiple myeloma is not one disease, but about ten different diseases, all producing identical symptoms. At the cellular level, my myeloma might be completely different from the myeloma of the person in the next chemo chair. The chemotherapy that works well for another person might have no effect on me.

I realized I was up against the Babe Ruth of cancers, so I told my doctors that (in baseball terminology) I wanted them to give me their "out" pitch—the pitch they could always count on to get the batter out. "Empty the medicine cabinet," I said. "Throw it all at me."

A Life Saved by Teamwork

Dr. Reynolds referred me to Dr. Yasser Khaled, a multiple myeloma and stem cell transplant specialist at Florida Hospital. By that time, I was seventy-one years old. The cutoff age for doing a stem cell transplant was sixty-five. The transplant procedure takes a heavy toll on the cardiovascular system, and it can trigger a heart attack or stroke in those who are not in good physical condition. Dr. Khaled waived the age limit in my case because of my overall good health. I had always worked out, run marathons, watched my diet, and avoided alcohol and tobacco, so my hard work had earned me an exemption.

I wondered if the stem cell transplant wasn't just a last-ditch effort with little chance of success. So I asked Dr. Khaled, "How many stem cell transplants have you done?"

"Three hundred."

"How many have been successful?"

"Three hundred."

"Are you saying your success rate is 100 percent?"

"That's exactly what I'm saying."

"How is that possible?"

"I choose my patients very carefully."

It wasn't that he was concerned about maintaining a perfect box score. He was simply not about to inflict a procedure on me that would likely kill me.

Dr. Khaled performed the complex process of harvesting nearly five million healthy stem cells from my bloodstream. It was not painful, but it was tedious. Dr. Khaled's team placed the harvested stem cells in cold storage, then they hit me with two massive blasts of chemo to destroy the remaining cancer cells in my blood marrow. Then they infused the healthy stem cells back into my body, where they multiplied and produced new blood cells.

At the end of the scariest year of my life, God gave me a miracle. My numbers came down. I was in remission at last. I now celebrate three birthdays every year—my physical birthday on May 3, 1940; my spiritual birthday when I committed my life to God on February 22, 1968; and my cancer remission birthday, February 10, 2012. Nearly five years after telling Dr. Reynolds that my daily theme would be "The Mission Is Remission," I can safely say, "Mission accomplished."

I'm alive today by the grace of God, and my life was saved by teamwork.

This mission was not accomplished by any one doctor working alone. Each doctor had a part to play, and so did each nurse and every other medical professional involved in my case. And so did all the researchers who developed the drugs, the procedures, the infusion devices, and on and on. My wife, Ruth, who accompanied me and took notes on everything the doctor told me, was part of the team. All my family members were part of the team. So was every member of the Orlando Magic organization, along with the incredibly supportive central Florida community.

And then there's Audra Hollifield, the Orlando Magic's human resources director. She practically dragged me to that physical assessment, where the blood test picked up the abnormal protein in my blood. I thought I was too busy to take a whole day for a physical exam, and I tried to get out of it. If not for Audra's insistence, I might not be here now to tell you the story.

The point is this: I am alive today because of teamwork. A medical staff is a team, and the principles of teamwork are essential to the practice of medicine. Business writer William A. Cohen explains how medical teamwork functions:

> Peter Drucker found an interesting phenomenon in investigating the procedures in a well-run hospital. Doctors, nurses, x-ray technicians, pharmacologists, pathologists, and other health care practitioners all worked together to accomplish a single object. Frequently he saw several working on the same patient under emergency conditions. Seconds counted. Even a minor slip could prove fatal. Yet, with a minimum amount of conscious command or control by any one individual, these medical teams worked together toward a common end and followed a common plan of action under the overall direction of a doctor.[1]

That's a concise description of the power of teamwork. On every medical team, each individual employs his or her talent and skill, which intersects with a passion for saving lives—and the result is *life*. For me, the result is remission. I'm so glad my doctors and nurses are so talented and so passionate about the work they do.

Multiplied Talent, Super-Sized Passion

There's no substitute for the power of teamwork. A team is a group of diverse people, with diverse personalities and diverse sets of talents and skills, who focus their talent and passion on a single goal. We are social creatures. We are designed to meet challenges and achieve goals through teamwork. As Duke University basketball coach Mike Krzyzewski has said, "People want to be on a team. They want to be part of something bigger than themselves. They want to be in a situation where they feel that they are doing something for the greater good."[2]

If you want to achieve the highest heights of success, if you want to multiply your talent and passion times ten or a hundred or a thousand, you need to think "Teamwork!" A team is one of the greatest of all human inventions. I have seen teamwork break down cultural barriers, racial barriers, religious barriers, and class barriers. I have seen people come together and unite as one, people who, apart from a team environment, would have no reason to be in the same room together.

On a team, there is no white or black, no Christian or Jew or Muslim, no rich or poor, no urban or rural—there is only the team. When a player looks at his teammates, he doesn't see skin color or any other superficial distinction. The only color teammates see is the color of the jersey.

Retired football coach Bill Curry was the chief architect of the Georgia State University football program from 2008 to 2012, and he also coached at Georgia Tech, Alabama, and Kentucky. Bill calls teamwork "the miracle of the huddle" because when players fuse themselves together as a team, their individual differences disappear. He explains:

> The huddle includes black America. The huddle includes Caucasian America. The huddle includes the liberal, the conservative, the Northerner, the Southerner, the East Coast guy and the West Coast guy, the city guy and the country guy. . . . That's the miracle of team. The miracle of team lasts forever. I've seen racists reformed. I've seen guys from south-central Los Angeles and country boys from the hills of eastern Kentucky who were raised to hate each other's guts—I've seen them become brothers for life. I've seen those very people invite each other home for Thanksgiving, thereby transforming the lives of the parents, all because of our game.[3]

One of the most important byproducts of teamwork is *love*—not that warm and fuzzy emotion people mistakenly call love, but an authentic *decision* to love one's teammates by seeking the best for them. We can choose to love our teammates, even if we are angry with them or don't like them.

Dusty Baker had a long career in baseball as an outfielder, primarily with the Dodgers and Braves, and he's now the manager of the Washington Nationals. His philosophy of teamwork was shaped by his service in the United States Marine Corps. In the Corps, every Marine looks out for his fellow Marines. Baker says a Marine will risk everything to save his teammate's life "even if you don't like him and he doesn't like you. That's teamwork."[4]

Baker is telling us that teamwork is powered by love. You don't have to *like* your teammate, but you do have to love him. Whether your teammate is a fellow soldier, a fellow player on your team, a member of your family, a fellow member of your church, or one of the doctors or nurses on your medical team, love is the greatest force of all.

I've often thought that we could solve most of our social problems if we stopped thinking in terms of us versus them, black versus white, citizen versus police, rich versus poor, Republican versus Democrat—and we started thinking of everyone in America as our teammate. What if we practiced "the miracle of the huddle" on a national basis? What if we began loving the people we don't like? Patrick Lencioni, author of *The Five Dysfunctions of a Team*, put it this way:

> Our society celebrates the individual. The Hall of Fame athlete gazes at us from the cover of *Sports Illustrated*. The corporate CEO looks confidently at us from the cover of *Forbes* or *BusinessWeek*.
>
> But when the game is over and all the points are on the scoreboard—or when the sales are totaled and the annual report goes to press—what stands out and endures is the accomplishment of the team. It's the amazing realization that human beings working together have accomplished far more than the sum of their individual efforts and abilities. Why? Because they committed themselves to something larger than themselves.
>
> They achieved greatness as a team.[5]

Teamwork happens when a just-right mixture of talents and personalities comes together, coalescing around a single goal with an intense passion. When the great talents of that team intersect with extreme passion for winning, that team will find its sweet spot. The result will be exciting performances, extreme victory, and rafters festooned with championship banners.

At the heart of every successful team is a concept called *synergy*. This word comes from the Greek *sunergos*, which means "working together" (from *sun*, "together," and *ergon*, "work"). In a team environment, synergy is the interaction between two or more teammates in such a way that their combined impact exceeds the sum of their individual strengths.

I've seen situations (and I'm sure you've seen them, too) where a manager or a teacher or a coach gathers a group of people together, assigns a task to them, and tells them, "You're a team." And it's obvious to everyone that they are not a team at all. They lack that mystical synergistic *something* that would bind them together into a genuine team.

It's as if you went down to the auto parts store, bought thousands of dollars' worth of car parts, and dumped them on your driveway. What do you have on your driveway? Is it a car? Of course not. It's just a collection of parts. In order to be a car, those parts have to be the right parts, and they have to be properly assembled. And in order for it to function, the car must have fuel in the tank.

In the same way, you can't just throw a bunch of people together and call them a "team." To be a team, they have to be the right people, with just the right mixture of talents and personality traits, and they have to be properly assembled. Equally important, in order to function as a team, they must be fueled by passion.

When you truly have a team, you can sense the synergy. The talent, passion, and intensity of your team far exceeds the sum of its parts. A team with synergy functions cohesively, thinking and acting as one, achieving more than anyone has any right to expect.

One of the most important ingredients in team synergy is a team attitude. As human beings we are 97 percent water—the rest is attitude. Do we think "me"—or "we"? Are we passionate about the goal? Are we willing to sacrifice and subordinate our individual ambitions for the good of the team? When the team truly begins to think as one and function as one, magic happens.

Legendary Celtics center Bill Russell described the sublime emotional experience when synergy happens—that amazing moment when everything just seems to work:

> Every so often, a Celtic game would heat up so that it would become more than a physical or mental game. It would be magical. The feeling is difficult to describe. And I certainly never talked about it when I was playing. When it happened, I could feel my play rise to a new level. . . .
>
> The game would move so fast that every fake, cut, and pass would be surprising—and yet nothing could surprise me. It was almost as if we were playing in slow motion. During those spells, I could almost sense how the next play would develop and where the next shot would be taken.[6]

I have experienced that same sense of being completely synchronized with my teammates, of feeling everything working together in harmony, like the blended chords of a symphony. People have described that same experience of synergy in many different settings—emergency responders working together in a crisis, dancers blending their talents on a stage, an ensemble of actors harmonizing their talents in a play. They have achieved, on a team level, that perfect intersection of great talent and great passion, and together they have found their synergistic sweet spot.

Peter Senge, senior lecturer at the MIT Sloan School of Management and author of *The Fifth Discipline*, wrote, "When a team becomes more aligned, a commonality of direction emerges, and individual energies harmonize. There is less wasted energy. In fact, a resonance or synergy develops like the coherent light of a laser rather than the incoherent and scattered light of a light bulb. There is a commonality of purpose, a shared vision, an understanding of how to complement one another's efforts."[7]

Teamwork has been one of the overarching themes of my life since I was a boy. I have always loved the shared excitement of victory, the shared consolation in defeat, and the sense of loyalty, mutual support, and love that teammates have for one another. For more than half a century, from my school days through college and throughout my professional career, I have lived in a team environment. In my family, I have always taught the biblical teamwork principle that comes to us from wise King Solomon: "Though one may be overpowered, two can defend themselves. A cord of three strands is not quickly broken."[8]

Teamwork multiplies and synergizes our individual talents. Teamwork intensifies and super-sizes our passion. Team spirit is one of the highest and noblest expressions of the human spirit.

I recently had a conversation with sportswriter Dan Ewald, who covered the 1975 World Series for the *Detroit News*. ESPN ranked this contest between the Cincinnati Reds and the Boston Red Sox as the second-greatest World Series ever played.

Game six at Fenway Park was played on a gray, cloudy day. It was an intense twelve-inning battle filled with unforgettable moments: the game-tying three-run homer by Red Sox pinch hitter Bernie Carbo in the eighth; Cincinnati reliever Will McEnaney pitching out of a bases-loaded situation; and Red Sox right fielder Dwight Evans making an epic eleventh-inning catch to rob Joe Morgan of a go-ahead home run. Cincinnati Reds manager Sparky Anderson set a World Series record for most pitchers used in a single game.

In the bottom of the twelfth, Boston's Carlton Fisk hit a walk-off home run down the line that stayed just fair. It gave the Red Sox a 7–6 win, and sent the series to a deciding seventh game. It was a crushing loss for Sparky Anderson—but to his amazement, he saw his star hitter, Pete Rose, jabbering excitedly, looking for all the world as if the Reds had just won.

Sparky couldn't understand how Pete Rose could be so excited and upbeat after a twelfth-inning loss in a World Series game. "Pete," Sparky said, "what's wrong with you?"

"Skip," Rose replied, "that's the best World Series game anyone will ever be in."

Sparky could only shake his head as he walked glumly to the clubhouse at Fenway. Later in the locker room, Pete Rose clapped Sparky on the back and said, "Cheer up, Skip. Tomorrow night is going to be the most amazing game of our careers."

"Sure, Pete," Sparky said grudgingly. "Whatever you say." But Sparky was still in the dumps.

The next day, October 22, 1975, Cincinnati went scoreless for five innings, then dramatically came from behind to win game seven, 4–3, and the World Series. Just as Pete Rose had promised, it was one of the most amazing games of Sparky's career.

When Sparky lost game six, he lost his confidence for game seven. But even a heartbreaking twelfth-inning loss couldn't dampen the passion, enthusiasm, and confidence of Pete Rose. For the rest of his days, Sparky Anderson never stopped talking about Pete Rose and his unquenchable passion for the game.

That's the beauty and power of teamwork. Our teammates make up for what we lack. Their talents compensate for the talents we lack, and when we are down, their passion lifts us up again. If you want to experience the highest, most rewarding success of all, you'll find it as you and your teammates merge your talents, pool your passion, and achieve great things together.

Team Up with People Who Complement You

The people in your life have an enormous influence on how you express your passion, utilize your talent, and pursue your dreams and goals of success. While it's important to have people around you who share your passion and affirm your talent, it's also important to have people in your life who will tell you the hard truths, who will provide talents and perspectives you lack—in short, people who will complement you.

The most successful coach of all time, in any sport, at any level, was the late UCLA men's basketball coach John Wooden. His advice was: "Whatever you do in life, surround yourself with smart people who'll argue with you."[9]

Veteran screenwriter and film producer Andrew Stanton has been a writer and/or director on a number of mega-successful Pixar animated films, including all three *Toy Story* films, *Monsters, Inc.*, *A Bug's Life*, *Finding Nemo*, and *WALL-E*. Stanton agrees that excellence and success come from having people around you who supply what you lack—including, at times, an opposing point of view. "Working at Pixar," he said, "you learn the really honest, hard way of making a great movie, which is to surround yourself with people who are much smarter than you, much more talented than you, and incite constructive criticism; you'll get a much better movie out of it. It's hard, it's never fun, you'll hear a lot of things you don't want to hear, and you'll fall down a lot, but I've only ever had greatness come out of that process."[10]

Surround yourself with people who will tell you the truth, who will even oppose you for your own good instead of telling you what you want to hear. Assemble a team of people representing a diversity of talents and abilities, all focused on a single unified goal. If you want to write a book or paint a canvas, all you need is one person with one talent. If you want to start a business or a charitable organization, you'll need a few more people. If you want to build a championship team, a business empire, or a rocket to Mars, you're going to need a very big team. You're going to need many people with many different skill sets and talents.

One of the most beneficial ways of joining forces with others is by finding another talented person who supplies what we lack and who lacks what we supply. This kind of reciprocal, complementary relationship has been the foundation of many highly successful partnerships and business ventures. The worst partnerships are composed of two people who are exactly alike. It does you no good to join forces with someone who has the same strengths as you—and the same weaknesses.

Susan Cain, author of *Quiet: The Power of Introverts in a World That Can't Stop Talking*, says that one of the most dynamic business relationships is a partnership between an introvert and an extrovert:

> The two types need each other. Many successful ventures are the result of effective partnerships between introverts and extroverts. The famously charismatic Steve Jobs teamed up with powerhouse introverts at crucial points in his career at Apple, cofounding the company with the shy Steve Wozniak and bequeathing it to its current CEO, the quiet Tim Cook. And the three-time Olympic-gold-winning rowing pair Marnie McBean and Kathleen Biddle were a classic match of dynamic firecracker (McBean) and steely determination (Biddle).[11]

Other examples abound. High school chums Ben Cohen and Jerry Greenfield joined forces to open their first ice-cream shop in 1978. Jerry, the introvert, manufactured the product and ran the store. Ben, the extrovert, went out and marketed the Ben and Jerry's brand. Together, Ben and Jerry were an unbeatable team.

We see the same pattern in the Microsoft Corporation, where Bill Gates (an extroverted marketing genius and deal maker) joined forces with Paul Allen (an introverted manager and tech innovator). The pattern appears again at Hewlett-Packard, where cofounders David Packard (driven extrovert) and William Hewlett (easygoing introvert) were an unbeatable team.

My friend Rich DeVos, the Orlando Magic co-owner, partnered with Jay Van Andel to found Amway. Rich was the extroverted outside salesman, while Jay was the introvert who developed products and managed the business. Rich and Jay magnified each other's strengths and compensated for each other's weaknesses—and in the process, they built a multilevel marketing empire.

Perhaps the greatest example of an ultra-successful complementary partnership was the longtime relationship between Walt Disney and his brother Roy. Walt was the imaginative, extroverted genius while Roy was the pragmatic, introverted financial brain of the operation.

Back in the 1930s, when the Disney studio was housed in a modest compound of buildings on Hyperion Avenue in Los Angeles, Walt and his writers and animators would often relax with a sandlot baseball game on the studio grounds. There is a home movie that was filmed during one of those games showing Walt at bat, hamming it up for the camera with all the enthusiasm of a classic extrovert. Then the camera pans over toward Walt's brother Roy, standing on the sidelines. After a few seconds, Roy becomes aware that the camera lens is trained on him, and he quickly steps back out of the frame—a typically introverted move.

That little bit of home movie footage speaks volumes about the partnership between Walt and Roy, two men who couldn't have been more different and who depended on each other for their mutual success.[12]

Who do you need to make your vision come true? Who is that special individual who supplies what you lack and lacks what you supply? Teamwork is the key to multiplying your talent and maximizing your passion. Merge your strengths with the talent and passion of someone who complements you. Then go out and conquer the world.

8

Guiding Others to Their Success Intersection

> If a child is to keep alive his inborn sense of wonder, he needs the companionship of at least one adult who can share it, rediscovering with him the joy, excitement, and mystery of the world we live in.
>
> **RACHEL CARSON**, writer and environmentalist

WHEN I WAS MUCH YOUNGER, and our house was full of children (four birth children and fourteen by international adoption), we started each day with breakfast together. Every morning at about seven o'clock, the children would come dragging in and take their places around our sixteen-foot-long dining room table. We put out the cold cereal and milk, and we'd have a morning devotional, and sometimes I'd pose a question to get their brains stirring.

One morning I said, "Twenty years from now, what are you going to remember about your dear old dad?" That's a dangerous question. You never know what the answer might be.

On that particular morning, my kids formed little buzz groups around the table, discussing the question in whispers among themselves. Finally, my son David put his hand up and said, "Dad, we're going to remember that you are always motivating us."

I chuckled. It was true. In addition to motivating them to keep their rooms clean or do their homework, I continually urged them to discover their talents and max them out.

My children are all adults now, and I have fifteen grandchildren—and I'm motivating a whole new generation, my children's children. One day, they'll look back on their old granddad, and they'll answer that question the same way David did—I was always motivating them and urging them to focus their talents and energize their talents with passion. Let me tell you about what one of my children did with her God-given talent and with all the motivational messages I imparted over the years.

My daughter Karyn has been musically inclined since age three. She's always loved singing, especially if you put a microphone in her hand. She performed often during her school years and on into college, where she won the Miss University of Florida pageant with a singing performance.

After college, she worked in the real estate and insurance fields, and it seemed as if music had taken a backseat in her life. She seemed to be happy in her business career. Only later did I find out that she wasn't happy at all.

One day in 2007, she said, "Dad, I'm taking you out to dinner. We need to talk."

So we sat down to dinner at McCormick and Schmick's, and Karyn handed me a framed photo of the two of us together, which I now keep on my desk. She also gave me a card she had written. I had to dab at my eyes in order to read it:

Daddy—

On one of my flights to Philadelphia, I was overcome with the urge to get out a piece of paper and write down everything that I've learned from you. Here's what I came up with:

1. *Be good to people.*
2. *Enjoy your life.*
3. *Wear your seat belt.*
4. *Life is all about relationships and collecting friends.*
5. *Work hard—every day!*
6. *Take care of your body.*
7. *Exercise your mind.*
8. *Dare to be big.*
9. *There are no giants out there.*
10. *The world will take care of the jerks.*
11. *Love the Lord—He's with you on the mountains as well as in the valleys.*

So Dad, as I'm embarking on this very exciting but very scary journey, I want to thank you for everything you have taught me. I am the person I am today because of the example you set for me. I feel prepared to go out and fight for what I want because you taught me to believe in myself. I love you more than life itself, and I am SO proud to be your daughter.

Now it's time for me to go and make you proud!!!

I love you!
Karyn

I looked at her in bewilderment and said, "It sounds like you're leaving."

"Yes, I'm leaving Orlando. I'm leaving my home."

"Where are you going?"

"I'm going to Nashville. I finally realize that the only goal in life I really care about is my music. I've got to give it a shot."

"Karyn, do you know anybody there?"

"No, Daddy. Not a soul."

"You know, thousands of people go to Nashville every year and try to make it in the music business. Most of them have a lot of talent, but they never achieve their dreams. I'm not trying to discourage you, but I want you to know that it won't be easy."

"I know all that," she said. "But I'm leaving tomorrow."

She had tears in her eyes, but also a gleam of excitement. She was doing what I had taught her to do—what I had always encouraged her and her brothers and sisters to do: dream big dreams. Take risks—not reckless gambles, but calculated risks. Live the adventure. Dare to be big.

I'll admit that a part of me wanted to protect her from hurt and disappointment. But I was also incredibly proud of her, knowing she had absorbed all those fatherly pep talks, and now she was putting it into action. She was setting out on the adventure of a lifetime, and no matter how it turned out, she'd have no regrets.

Karyn left Florida on July 17, 2007. My wife, Ruth, and I blanketed her with prayer. Karyn later told me she cried all the way to Nashville. But she found a place to live, and she landed the traditional job of the as-yet-undiscovered singer, waiting tables. She found out where all the songwriters congregated, and she met a man named Brian White, a songwriter-musician-producer. He opened doors for her and—long story short—she eventually brought Brian to Orlando to meet us. Today, they are married.

In 2011, Karyn signed with Inpop Records, which is also the label of such artists as the Newsboys, Jaci Velasquez, and Mat Kearney. She released her first full-length studio album, *Only You*, in 2012—the same year she was selected as one of Billboard's "Best Bets." She made her debut with the Grand Ole Opry in December 2014 and recorded a duet with Mac Powell of Third Day. She also tours with comedienne Chonda Pierce, "the Queen of Clean."

Our job as parents—or teachers or leaders or employers or friends—is to help others find their success intersection. Our job is to encourage and motivate the people around us (especially our own children) to dream big dreams, take risks, live the adventure, and dare to be big.

Helping Them Live Undefeated Lives

Parents don't always realize how talented their children are.

Chinese-American actor James Hong has appeared in more than five hundred TV and motion picture roles, going back to the 1950s. He has appeared in such films as *Big Trouble in Little China*, *Blade Runner*, *Black Widow*, *Chinatown*, and (as a voice actor) Disney's *Mulan*. Yet his parents—and especially his father—opposed his dream of becoming an actor.

Hong told an interviewer that his father wanted him to be a civil engineer. "My parents thought being an actor would be, in essence, lowering myself," he said. They viewed acting as a demeaning career, because actors openly demonstrate emotions—and in his parents' culture, people were expected to control and hide their emotions. So James Hong concealed his aspirations from his mother and father.

Though James Hong's parents discouraged his talent and his passion for acting, Hong gives credit to his parents for his acting talent. "I've often wondered how and why did I become an actor," he said. "Where did I get the so-called talent to express myself? And I look back and I see that my mother was very animated, I can remember that she used to, what she called *bei zhu*. The Chinese love to read books out loud, and she used to sing with many tones sort of like poetry—making poetry of the whole book. I could hear the expression in her voice. Also, my father was a speaker. He got up and spoke in front of audiences."

So a talent for performing was in his genetic makeup. "I inherited those genes and I simply channeled those so-called genes and talents into performing arts. They had it, but they weren't actors in that sense as professional people. . . . [I] took those performing arts talents and multiplied them into a career."[1]

Though James Hong's parents opposed his dream of becoming an actor, he clung to his memories of his parents reading aloud, singing in a poetic style, and speaking before audiences. Those memories connected him to the traditions of his past—and to his future in Hollywood.

How many talented and gifted children live out their lives never discovering their talents, and never knowing what kind of contribution they could have made? As parents, teachers, and leaders, we have an obligation to help people, young and old, discover their talent and find their sweet spot in life.

I once interviewed José Abreu, then secretary of transportation for the state of Florida. I knew he had children and was coaching Little League, so I asked him if he made an intentional effort to help his children and his players discover their talents and abilities.

"Absolutely," he told me. "Whether at home, or when I'm coaching a team of Little Leaguers, or I'm leading a team of adults at the Florida Department of Transportation, my task is essentially the same. My job is to uncover talent and build team unity, so that everyone on the team can use their talent to achieve the team goals.

"I want everyone on the team to know his or her role and objectives, and I want them to be disciplined in working together to achieve those objectives. I used to coach my son's Little League team in Hialeah. Nobody thought our team had the talent to go undefeated, yet there was one season in which we won every game we played. They had the talent. My job was to help them discover it.

"During one of the games that season, I overheard a parent of one of the boys on an opposing team say, 'Look at those kids!'—referring to our team. 'Look at the way they follow instructions! I don't know if I'd want my son to be on his team. They look more like synchronized sewing machines than real people.'

"That parent meant it as a disparaging remark. He said our kids acted like robots. But they weren't robots. They were a team! They took direction, they coordinated their talents and abilities, and they acted as one. I took it as a compliment."

José Abreu motivated his players to use their talents to achieve their goals. As a result, his team went undefeated. When we help our children, our students, or the people around us to discover their talent and pursue their passion, they can live undefeated lives as well.

As we look for the hidden talent in others, we will find that some have a latent ability to be leaders. Some have gifts of public speaking. Some have athletic abilities. Some will have artistic or literary talent. Some are drawn to mathematics, science, or business.

Motivational consultant David Spitzer observes that most people "have a great many strengths that they can rarely get to use. Strengths can be job skills and knowledge, general abilities, personality characteristics. Research has found that every person can do at least one thing better than any other 10,000 people."[2]

Our challenge is to study our children, students, employees, and coworkers, and help them discover the talents they possess.

Steps to Helping Others Discover Their Talent

Everyone has talents and abilities they don't even recognize. Here are a number of practical steps you can take to help children, teenagers, and adults discover their hidden talents.

1. *Share your own experiences.* Talk about the lessons you've learned in childhood and adolescence, and in your

career. Share both triumphs and failures, so that the people you influence can learn the principles that lead to success, and the steps for recovering from failure. How did you discover your talents? When did you become aware of your purpose in life? How did you go about setting your life goals? Tell your story and share your experiences with others.

I once interviewed Dr. Pamela M. Brill, author of *The Winner's Way*. She told me her parents helped her to discover her values, her interests, and her talents. "My dad was orphaned at four," she said. "He was raised on the farm of his foster parents during the Great Depression. He got to play baseball when he was a boy, and he also learned to fly the crop-dusting planes. After graduating from high school, Dad traveled to China with a bunch of other young mavericks, and they became the Chinese Air Force—the original Flying Tigers who defended China against attack by Japan before America officially entered the war. My mother worked in Washington, DC, as an assistant to the quartermaster general, living in a boarding house for young women.

"Throughout my life, my parents told me stories from their early lives, or stories about people they had known. Most of those stories had to do with virtue, values, and character. I constantly heard such statements as, 'Time is life—don't waste it,' and 'Follow your heart but use your head.' I learned the importance of hard work, self-sacrifice, courage, believing in myself, and living with passion and purpose.

"When I was twelve, Dad gave me two books to read—*PT 109*, the story of John F. Kennedy's heroism in World War II, and Dale Carnegie's *How to Win Friends and Influence People*. I'm grateful that my parents were true heroes and role models, and that they shared their stories with me."

You've spent your lifetime learning lessons and accumulating wisdom. Now it's time to help others to find their talent and purpose in life. Share your wisdom. Tell your stories.

2. *Turn every experience into a learning experience.* Examples include playing board games and outdoor sports together, taking walks and talking together, and letting young people help in the kitchen. All of these experiences can become opportunities for you to learn about your children, and for your children to discover their own talents and interests. Be alert to special moments when you can talk about character, values, hard work, perseverance, and other qualities that lead to success.

The more time you spend with the people you influence, the better you will understand them—and the more abilities and talents you will see in them. Observe closely. Tune in to their interests. Listen to their questions. Notice the activities that they excel in and enjoy.

Different abilities and talents will emerge at different stages of their lives. They will demonstrate new talents as they explore new activities and experiences. Take special notice when they show signs of advanced ability or mastery in certain skills.

3. *Encourage unselfish service to others.* One of the best ways both children and adults can discover their talents and abilities is by volunteering to serve others. People who volunteer at a homeless shelter, a veterans' home, or a rescue mission frequently discover talents and abilities they never realized they had.

I once received an email from a father, Tom Walsh. At the time, he had two sons, ages two and four, with a third child on the way. He told me that after reading my book *Souls of Steel*, he was inspired to begin teaching his sons how to unselfishly serve others.

One Saturday morning, he took his boys to a bagel store for breakfast, and then they went to a nearby nursing home to visit the residents. He went to the front desk and told the receptionist that he and the boys would like to visit someone.

"Who have you come to visit?" the receptionist asked.

"Anyone," Tom replied. "I'm sure there's someone here who could use a visit."

The nursing home staff invited Tom and his boys to wander around and talk to people. Tom's four-year-old, George, boldly walked up to the residents, put out his hand, and said, "Hi! My name is George. It's nice to meet you!"

The residents were charmed by Tom and his boys. In the process, Tom was helping his sons to discover hidden talents for serving others, for making people happy, for being assertive and reaching out to others. As these boys gave a lift to the residents, they also practiced their social skills, increased their confidence, and overcame their shyness. It's never too early to start teaching children to help others.

There are many ways young people can use their talents to serve others. Children with artistic talent can draw pictures, children with musical talent can perform, teens with the ability to wash cars or mow lawns can help raise funds for charities.

Marian Wright Edelman founded the Children's Defense Fund in 1973 to assist poor children in America. She once told me about the importance of encouraging young people to serve others and discover their gifts and abilities.

"My parents and the other adults in my community," she said, "taught me that faith is reflected in daily service. You got up every morning and you did what you had to do. You got up every time you fell down and tried as many times as needed to get it done right. My elders had grit. They tried to be good role models and expose us to examples of character.

"My role models taught me that the world had a lot of problems; that black people had an extra lot of problems, but that we were obligated to struggle and solve those problems. Being poor was no excuse for not achieving. I learned that service to others is the rent we pay for living. It's the very purpose of life and not something you do in your spare time."

As we encourage young people to do works of service, they will discover depths of talent and ability they never imagined they had.

4. *Avoid being judgmental when people try something new*. This is especially true in our role as parents. If a child takes a risk and explores some new area of talent, then feels criticized for failing, he or she may never dare to risk again.

Psychotherapist Susan Forward tells the story of a woman named Vicki who came to her for counseling. A professional woman in her thirties, Vicki was paralyzed with self-doubt. Her boss had just offered to pay her way through an MBA program, but Vicki was panicked at the thought of taking a risk and failing. Dr. Forward soon uncovered the source of Vicki's fears: a critical and judgmental mother.

Vicki believed her mother meant well, even when she spoke harshly. "Ballet recitals were the worst," Vicki recalled. "I'll never forget one recital when I was about twelve. I thought I'd done pretty well, but my mom came backstage and said—in front of the whole class—'You danced like a hippo.' I just wanted to sink through the floor."

Dr. Forward concluded that Vicki's mother was sending her confusing, contradictory messages. "On one hand," Forward said, "she urged her daughter to excel, while on the other hand she told her how terrible she was. Vicki always felt off balance, never sure whether she was doing anything right. When she thought she'd done well, her mother deflated her; when she thought she'd done poorly, her mother told her she couldn't do any better. At a time when Vicki should have been building self-confidence, her mother was knocking her down."

The result? Vicki gave up on herself, on her talent, on her goals. "For so many years," Vicki said, "I didn't do a lot of things, even things I really liked, because I was afraid of being humiliated. After I grew up, I kept hearing her voice, just putting me down. . . . She made me feel like such a loser. It hurt so bad."[3]

Many years ago, I had a speaking engagement in Hickory, North Carolina, and had a chance to visit with my longtime friend Jim Raugh. He reminisced about his days as a high school pitcher for the Haverford School in Pennsylvania. He recalled one game in particular, Haverford versus Friends Central—a sixteen-inning marathon that Haverford won, 1–0.

"I pitched a perfect game for ten innings," Jim told me. "But in the eleventh, I walked my first hitter. After the game, my father came up to me and said, 'Why did you walk that hitter in the eleventh?' I had pitched ten perfect innings and we had won the game. But all he could think about was that one walk in the eleventh. I'm almost sixty years old, and I can still hear his words in my mind like it was yesterday. Isn't that funny? That's what I remember most about that game: 'Why did you walk that hitter in the eleventh?'"

Jim didn't need to have his dad on his back. He needed cheers and praise for a job well done. We can't help others excel by destroying their self-confidence. We can't help others discover their talent by making them feel like losers.

Let's praise not only performance, but perseverance. Let's affirm not only success, but striving. Let's build up our children, our students, and the people around us. In the process we'll see their talents emerge and bloom.

Encourage Passion in Others

Helping young people and grown-ups discover their hidden talent is only half the battle. The other half, of course, is helping them to discover their passion in life. I once interviewed Dom Capers, defensive coordinator of the Green Bay Packers. We talked about the importance of helping young people discover and pursue their passion.

"Young people who are passionate about their goals," Capers told me, "are the ones who will be tomorrow's leaders and achievers. Passion produces power and intensity. Young people who are passionate about what they do are competitive. They are ready to take on a challenge. They are eager to be held accountable so that they can step up their performance. They go above and beyond what is required of them. They have the courage and conviction to stay the course and battle their way through adversity. Passion is contagious. People who have that kind of passion can fire up an entire team to do incredible things."

Here are some ideas for igniting the passion of the people around you, especially your children and students:

1. *Expose young people to a variety of interests and experiences.* Let them discover and explore the activities they enjoy the most. Notice the activities they choose in their free time. The choices they make on their own will tell you a lot about their interests and passions.

My mother constantly exposed me to new experiences, from sports to the arts. She was a fanatic about reading good books, and she read aloud to me when I was little and had me read to her as I became old enough to read. As a result, I've been a compulsive reader throughout my life. Mom also took us to concerts, Broadway shows, museums, and zoos in New York and Philadelphia. I'll always be grateful for the rich and well-rounded childhood she gave me.

Provide as many different kinds of experiences as you can, and when young people show an interest in any given area, find a way to feed that interest. If a young person shows an aptitude for music, arrange for music lessons. If art, arrange for art lessons. Find a way to fan that spark of talent to a roaring blaze. Encourage them to practice, to have fun, to treat that interest as something to revel in and enjoy—a delight, not a chore. Be supportive of the hobbies, interests, and passions of that young person.

2. *Be an encourager.* Pablo Picasso once said, "Every child is an artist. The problem is how to remain an artist once we grow up."[4] Picasso understood the need to encourage passion in children so that they feel free to express their talent without being inhibited. Both children and adults need to

feel free to pursue their passions and their dreams. Whether we are parenting children, coaching young adults, or leading an organization of adults, we need to cheer them on, fire up their passion, and let them know we're on their side, win, lose, or draw.

My father, Jim Williams, was my biggest fan when I was a boy. He was supportive of me and my goals, and he stressed the importance of hard work in achieving our dreams. For six years, I had a paper route, and Dad was always up with me at six a.m., driving the car while I threw the papers.

My dad was always whooping, cheering, and taking home movies at my games. He'd tell everybody, "That's my boy!" Looking back, I wish I had been more grateful for his enthusiasm and support. Fact is, I often felt embarrassed that he was so loud and demonstrative in front of my friends. I realize now that there are a lot of kids who would do anything for just a tiny scrap of attention from their mom and dad. I was fortunate to be so loved and have parents who encouraged me. They let me pursue my dreams, they told me it was okay to make mistakes, and they helped me to discover and recognize my talents.

As parents, teachers, employers, and leaders, we need to encourage those who are within our sphere of influence. Let's cheer them on and encourage them to take risks for their talent. When they suffer setbacks and disappointments, let's help them put a positive frame around that negative experience, so they will treat it as a learning experience instead of a disaster.

Instead of praising accomplishments and results, affirm them for character traits of diligence, self-discipline, self-motivation, perseverance, courage, and a commitment to excellence. If you only praise accomplishments, they might become "approval junkies" who get down on themselves when they lose or fail. Let them know that your approval is constant and your support is unconditional.

One of my early mentors was the great baseball owner and promoter Bill Veeck. He operated some legendary ball clubs—the Cleveland Indians, the St. Louis Browns, the Chicago White Sox, and the minor league Milwaukee Brewers. I met Bill in 1962 when I was twenty-two years old, and I often called him for advice and encouragement during my early career. After I completed my first year as general manager of the Spartanburg Phillies, I was feeling discouraged because our team didn't play well that season and finished near the bottom of the rankings.

I called Bill, and he listened patiently as I poured my heart out. Then he said, "Tell me, Pat—how many fans did you draw to the ballpark this season?" I told him we had brought in 114,000 people. "How many of them had a good time?" I said they all did. "Name one thing you could have done this summer to bring that much joy and entertainment to so many people." I couldn't think of a thing. "Pat," he said, "you never have to apologize for showing people a fun time."

By the time we finished talking, my outlook was transformed. I had been feeling like a failure. Bill convinced me I was a success. I had been doubting my talent for the job—and I had lost my passion. Bill made me feel like a superstar general manager. I will never forget the encouragement I received from Bill Veeck. True encouragers are never forgotten.

3. *Share stories of achievers and heroes.* Introduce children and adults to inspiring stories of people who are passionate

about accomplishing great things and helping others. Tell them about your own personal heroes. Ask them, "Who are your heroes? What made them special? What was their unique passion in life?" If they offer a superficial answer like "I just think he's cool" or "He's my hero because he's rich and famous," encourage them to think more deeply: "How do your heroes use their talent and passion to serve others?" It's important for them to choose their heroes well because people tend to become like the people they admire.

Former Dodgers general manager Buzzie Bavasi once told me that his hero was the great baseball executive Branch Rickey, who served as general manager of the St. Louis Cardinals, Brooklyn Dodgers, and Pittsburgh Pirates. Buzzie said, "I decided early on that I wanted to emulate Mr. Rickey. I made up my mind to win as many pennants as he did. And I did—largely because of the lessons I learned from watching his life. My advice to young people is to pick out a person that you respect and want to be like. Then, whenever you have to make an important decision, ask yourself what that hero would do in the same situation."

Our heroes don't have to be famous. In fact, local heroes and family heroes are often easier to learn from than celebrities. Heroes can be found in books, in newspaper stories, on the internet, in family histories—and sometimes heroes are within our reach. I recommend that, whenever possible, you *personally* introduce young people to flesh-and-blood heroes.

Years ago, I was catching in an old-timer's baseball game, and our first baseman was none other than Pete Rose. What a privilege to play on the same team as the man known as "Charlie Hustle." Yes, Pete has his flaws—we all do. But during his baseball career, Pete also won three World Series rings, three batting titles, and two Gold Gloves, and made seventeen All-Star appearances.

My three oldest boys—Jimmy, Bobby, and David—were teenagers at the time. They sat in the dugout during the game and rubbed shoulders with sports legends they had only seen on TV and baseball cards. Bobby was playing baseball in high school at the time, so I introduced him to Pete and said, "They called you 'Charlie Hustle.' Would you have a word of advice for Bobby about what 'hustle' means to you?"

Pete laughed. "Bobby, I never cared for that nickname 'Charlie Hustle.' I don't think of what I do as 'hustle.' I prefer the word 'enthusiasm.' I had so much fun playing the game that I couldn't help doing it well. I played with a heart full of enthusiasm every day. Once I got to the ballpark, I couldn't wait to hear 'Play ball!' I believe God gave me certain skills—not great skills, but good skills. You can't make it in this game on talent alone. But if you take the talent God gave you and add an intense passion and great enthusiasm, you just might have a special career."

Bobby has never forgotten those words—and neither have I. Today, Bobby enjoys a career in baseball management, and he approaches every day of his career with passion and enthusiasm. Heroes give people a standard to measure themselves against. Heroes inspire our passion and our enthusiasm. One of the best ways to ignite the passion of the people we influence is by introducing them to great heroes.

4. *Encourage a sense of wonder and curiosity.* To help your children, students, or the people you lead find their passion in life, encourage them to be sensitive to the amazing wonders of this world. Encourage them to continually deepen their

knowledge, widen their horizons, and seek out the wonder in everyday existence.

Put up a hummingbird feeder to encourage a fascination with nature. Encourage discussions of big ideas like the existence of God, the immortality of the soul, or the age and vastness of the universe. Turn off the TV, and go out on an August night and watch a meteor shower. Visit the woods, the science museum, a bird sanctuary, a butterfly farm, an aquarium, or a planetarium. Or get on a boat and go whale watching.

If a young person expresses an interest in writing, schedule a field trip to the home of a great author—Edith Wharton's estate in Lenox, Massachusetts, the Mark Twain House in Hartford, Connecticut, or John Steinbeck's home in Salinas, California. Is your young person interested in internet technology? Take a vacation trip to Silicon Valley and tour the headquarters of Google, Apple, and Facebook, see the home where Steve Jobs and Steve Wozniak built the first Apple computer, and visit the garage where Bill Hewlett and Dave Packard founded HP.

Whatever the interest and talent you see in people, find a creative approach to instilling a sense of wonder in them. In the process, you just might ignite a lifelong passion.

5. *Share your own passions.* The most influential role models children learn from are their own parents. The most influential role models students learn from are their teachers and professors. The most influential role models adults learn from are the leaders in their organizations or teams. If you seek to be an influence on young people or adults, if you want to ignite their passion for achieving great goals, then

share your passions with them. Let them know what fires you up, what energizes you, and the causes you care about more than anything in the world.

Malala Yousafzai is a Pashtun student from the Swat Valley in northwestern Pakistan. Her father, Ziauddin Yousafzai, named her after Malalai of Maiwand, a Pashtun woman who fought against the British in Afghanistan in 1880. Ziauddin has a passion for education that he instilled in Malala from an early age. He operated a school in Swat, a region of Pakistan where very few children attended school.

The Swat Valley has long been a stronghold of the fundamentalist Taliban, and the Taliban had forbidden girls to attend school. In 2009, as the Taliban's stranglehold on the Swat region intensified, twelve-year-old Malala began blogging under a pseudonym for the BBC Urdu service.

When Taliban thugs threatened Ziauddin, ordering him to close his school or face death, Ziauddin defied their commands. His daughter Malala wrote in her blog about the Taliban threats. During those tense days, the *New York Times* sent a film crew to Pakistan and produced a documentary about Malala, revealing her as the author of the BBC blog—and exposing her to the wrath of the Taliban.

On October 9, 2012, Malala and her classmates were bused to a nearby town to take their exams. As they were returning home, a Taliban hit squad halted the vehicle and a masked gunman stepped aboard and shouted, "Which one of you is Malala?" When Malala identified herself, the gunman opened fire, shooting Malala and two other girls. Malala was wounded in the head. The bullet was deflected down through her neck and lodged in her shoulder. The other two girls suffered less severe wounds.

Malala was taken to the hospital in critical condition. Pakistani doctors stabilized her, then airlifted her to Queen Elizabeth Hospital in Birmingham, England, a hospital specializing in treating war-related injuries. She received several surgeries and intensive rehab treatment, and was finally released in January 2013. She returned in February for a five-hour operation to restore hearing in one ear and reconstruct her damaged skull.

The Taliban had attempted to execute her for the "crime" of advocating education for Pakistani girls. The attempt on her life was condemned worldwide and protested throughout Pakistan. The National Assembly of Pakistan quickly passed the nation's first legislation guaranteeing free education for all.

In 2013, Malala and her father cofounded the Malala Fund, with the goal of raising awareness of the need for education for girls around the world. It was the fulfillment of the passionate dream of both Malala and her father, Ziauddin.

On her sixteenth birthday, July 12, 2013, Malala delivered a moving speech before the United Nations in New York. "The Taliban shot me," she said. "They shot my friends too. They thought that the bullets would silence us, but they failed. . . . I am the same Malala. My ambitions are the same. My hopes are the same. And my dreams are the same. Dear sisters and brothers, I am not against anyone. I do not even hate the Talib who shot me. . . . This is the forgiveness that I have learned from my father and from my mother. This is what my soul is telling me: be peaceful and love everyone."

The following year, on December 10, 2014, Malala was awarded the Nobel Peace Prize. She contributed all of her $1.1 million prize money to the creation of a new secondary school to serve the needs of Pakistani girls. The passion of Malala Yousafzai for a peaceful world, and the passion of her father, Ziauddin, for learning and education, proved even more powerful than a terrorist's bullet.[5]

What is your passion? What drives you toward your goals? Are you sharing your passion with your children, your students, and the people around you? Help them discover their talent. Inspire them to summon their passion. When their greatest talent intersects with their strongest passion, they will find their meaning, their purpose, and their sweet spot in life. And they will thank you.

Discover your talent. Ignite your passion. Identify talent and stir up passion in others. Believe in yourself. Find your sweet spot in life.

Change the world.

Notes

Chapter 1 Standing at the Intersection

1. Robert Tuchman, *Young Guns: The Fearless Entrepreneur's Guide to Chasing Your Dreams and Breaking Out on Your Own* (New York: AMACOM, 2009), 7–8.

2. Ibid., 8.

3. Ibid., 10.

4. Adapted from Jim Collins, "Tools—Discussion Guide," http://www.jimcollins.com/tools/discussion-guide.html.

5. Mike Dahl, "Rueben Martinez—A Life Well Read," Impact.fm, March 9, 2012, http://www.impact.fm/rueben-martinez-a-life-well-read/.

6. Mary Platt, "Rueben Martinez Named Chapman Fellow," *Orange County Register*, October 21, 2008, http://www.ocregister.com/articles/martinez-142461-community-chapman.html.

7. Ken Robinson, *Out of Our Minds: Learning to be Creative* (Chichester, West Sussex, UK: Capstone, 2011), 164–65.

8. G. Richard Shell, *Springboard: Launching Your Personal Search for Success* (New York: Penguin, 2013), 2.

9. Ibid., 8–9.

Chapter 2 Identify Your Talent

1. Paul Bear Bryant with John Underwood, *Bear: The Hard Life & Good Times of Alabama's Coach Bryant* (Chicago: Triumph Books, 2007), Kindle ed., chap. 33.

2. Harlan Ellison, *Edgeworks, Volume 3: The Harlan Ellison Hornbook / Harlan Ellison's Movie* (Stone Mountain, GA: White Wolf, 1997), 202–3.

3. Margaret Fuhrer, "Are You Ready for Some Football [Players in Ballet Class]?," *DanceSpirit Magazine*, September 26, 2013, http://www.dancespirit.com/margarets-musings/are-you-ready-for-some-football-players-in-ballet-class/.

4. Jason Moore, "Steelers Lineman Steve McLendon Mastering Ballet to Prevent Injuries," Atlanta Black Star, July 31, 2013, http://atlantablackstar.com/2013/07/31/steve-mclendon-ballet-dancing-prevent-injuries/.

5. BalletHub, "How Ballet Benefits Football Players," BalletHub.com, February 2, 2014, http://ballethub.com/ballet-benefits-football-players/.

6. See Jane Do staff, "Spotlight (Page 2)," SeeJaneDo.com, March 12, 2013, http://www.seejanedo.com/category/c12-everyday-women/page/2/.

7. Paul Hendrickson, *Hemingway's Boat: Everything He Loved in Life, and Lost, 1934–1961* (New York: Vintage / Random House, 2012), 145–46.

8. Ibid., 248.

9. Michael E. Haskew, *West Point 1915: Eisenhower, Bradley, and the Class the Stars Fell On* (Minneapolis: Zenith Press, 2014), 98.

Chapter 3 Identify Your Passion

1. William C. Rhoden, "Sports of the Times: For Mets, a Question of Talent or of Character?," *New York Times*, October 1, 2007, http://www.nytimes.com/2007/10/01/sports/baseball/01rhoden.html.

2. Bernice Napach, "Most Americans Not Happy at Work: Yahoo! Finance/Parade Survey," Yahoo! Daily Ticker, August 29, 2012, http://finance.yahoo.com/blogs/daily-ticker/most-americans-not-happy-yahoo-finance-parade-survey-112833013.html.

3. Art Lindsley, "How Do I Find My Calling?," Institute for Faith, Work & Economics, December 13, 2012, https://tifwe.org/how-do-i-find-my-calling/.

4. Martin Luther King Jr., ed. James M. Washington, *I Have a Dream—40th Anniversary Edition: Writings and Speeches That Changed the World* (San Francisco: HarperSanFrancisco, 1992), 20.

5. Michael S. Kavic, MD, "Surgery, Passion, and the Medical Student," *JSLS: Journal of the Society of Laparoendoscopic Surgeons*, July–September 1999, 169–70.

6. Condoleezza Rice, Commencement Address, Southern Methodist University, May 12, 2012, SMU.edu (transcript posted May 14, 2012), http://www.smu.edu/News/2012/commencement-Condoleezza-Rice-speech.

7. Michael Mink, "Jack Ramsay Had a Passion for Basketball that Won Out," *Investors Business Daily*, March 20, 2015, http://www.investors

.com/news/management/leaders-and-success/jack-ramsay-had-a-passion-for-basketball/.

8. Jason Cole, "Curtis Martin Reflects on Mother's Pain, Lack of Passion for Football at Hall of Fame," Yahoo Sports, August 5, 2012, http://sports.yahoo.com/news/nfl--curtis-martin-reflects-on-mother%E2%80%99s-pain--lack-of-passion-for-football-during-soul-baring-hall-speech.html; Jenny Vrentas, "Hall Of Fame Running Back Curtis Martin Never Liked Football, and He Hated New York and the Jets," *Star Ledger*, July 24, 2012, http://www.nj.com/jets/index.ssf/2012/07/curtis_martin_never_liked_foot.html; Bill Marsh Jr., "Four Keys to Injecting Passion and Purpose into Your Life—from an NFL Hall of Famer," BillMarshJr.com, November 14, 2013, http://www.billmarshjr.com/tag/curtis-martin/.

9. Drew Houston, Commencement Address, Massachusetts Institute of Technology, June 7, 2013, GraduationWisdom.com (posted January 7, 2014), http://www.graduationwisdom.com/speeches/0144-Drew-Houston-commencement-Speech-MIT-2013.htm.

10. Kevin Patra, "Ravens' John Urschel Begins PhD Program at MIT," NFL.com, February 1, 2016, http://www.nfl.com/news/story/0ap3000000630796/article/ravens-john-urschel-begins-phd-program-at-mit.

11. Kenneth Arthur, "Meet John Urschel, NFL Mathlete and Lover of Graph Laplacians," *Rolling Stone*, March 27, 2015, http://www.rollingstone.com/culture/features/meet-john-urschel-nfl-mathlete-and-lover-of-graph-laplacians-20150327.

12. Warren Berger, *A More Beautiful Question: The Power of Inquiry to Spark Breakthrough Ideas* (New York: Bloomsbury, 2014), 181.

13. Walter E. Fluker, *Ethical Leadership: The Quest for Character, Civility, and Community* (Minneapolis: Fortress Press, 2009), 170.

Chapter 4 Focus Your Talent

1. Chris Matthews, *Chris Matthews Complete Library E-book Box Set: Tip and the Gipper, Jack Kennedy, Hardball, Kennedy & Nixon, Now, Let Me Tell You What I Really Think, and American* (New York: Simon & Schuster, 2013), Kindle ed., chap. 9.

2. Faisal Hoque, "Why You Probably Aren't Investing Enough In Your Own Advancement," *Fast Company*, September 1, 2015, http://www.fastcompany.com/3050551/lessons-learned/why-you-probably-arent-investing-enough-in-your-own-advancement.

3. Daniel Goleman, *Focus: The Hidden Driver of Excellence* (New York: HarperCollins, 2013), 163.

4. Pete Hamill, *Piecework: Writings on Men & Women, Fools and Heroes, Lost Cities, Vanished Friends, Small Pleasures, Large Calamities, and How the Weather Was* (New York: Little, Brown, 1996), 253.

5. Gordon D'Angelo, *Vision: Your Pathway to Victory* (New York: Morgan James, 2012), Kindle ed., chap. 1.

6. Andy Stanley, *Visioneering: God's Blueprint for Developing and Maintaining Personal Vision* (New York: Random House, 1999), 9–10.

7. Rebecca Burn-Callander, "Exclusive interview: Sir Richard Branson," *Vision Magazine* (Vision.ae, Dubai), January 2014, http://vision.ae/focus/exclusive_interview_sir_richard_branson.

8. Ian O'Neill, "Branson Outlines His Vision for Virgin Galactic, Video Interview," Universe Today, January 22, 2008, http://www.universetoday.com/12529/branson-outlines-his-vision-for-virgin-galactic-video-interview/.

9. Richard Branson, "Richard Branson on the Power of Your People," Entrepreneur.com, January 4, 2011, http://www.nbcnews.com/id/40905058/ns/business-small_business/t/richard-branson-power-your-people/.

10. Ryan O'Reilly, *Shifting Gears: How to Harness Your Drive to Reach Your Potential and Accelerate Success* (New York: Morgan James, 2016), 79.

11. Dave McGillivray, "Dave McGillivray—Race Director, Motivator, World-Renowned Athlete, Philanthropist, Entrepreneur," Speaker biography, http://www.orangerunnersclub.org/docs/Dave_McGillivray_Bio.pdf.

12. Keith Dunnavant, *Bart Starr: America's Quarterback and the Rise of the National Football League* (New York: St. Martin's Press, 2011), 204.

13. Kristen Lamb, "Writing Tip #3—Talent Is Cheaper than Table Salt," Kristen Lamb's Blog, January 7, 2013, https://warriorwriters.wordpress.com/2013/01/07/writing-tip-3-talent-is-cheaper-than-table-salt/.

14. Tania Modic, "1996 USC Commencement Address," YouTube.com, accessed June 9, 2016, https://www.youtube.com/watch?v=2-bHacyrbN0.

15. Kathleen K. Reardon, "Courage as a Skill," *Harvard Business Review*, January 2007, https://hbr.org/2007/01/courage-as-a-skill.

16. Modic, "1996 USC Commencement Address."

17. Hoque, "Why You Probably Aren't Investing Enough In Your Own Advancement."

18. Deborah Morrison, "The One Thing That Truly Motivates Creative Talent—and How to Foster It," *Fast Company*, December 3, 2013, http://www.fastcocreate.com/3022240/the-one-thing-that-truly-motivates-creative-talent-and-how-to-foster-it.

19. Kim Alexis, *A Model for a Better Future* (Nashville: Thomas Nelson, 1999), Kindle ed.

20. John Wooden with Jack Tobin, *They Call Me Coach* (McGraw-Hill Education, 2003), 185.

Chapter 5 Focus Your Passion

1. Brian Jay Jones, *Jim Henson: The Biography* (New York: Ballantine, 2013), 76.

2. Scott S. Smith, "Jim Henson Turned His Muppets into Global Celebrities," *Investors Business Daily*, September 8, 2015, http://www.investors.com/news/management/leaders-and-success/jim-henson-invented-the-muppets/.

3. Jim Henson, *Wisdom from It's Not Easy Being Green and Other Things to Consider* (New York: Hyperion, 2005), Kindle ed., 25.

4. David Zahl, "The Gospel according to Jim Henson," *Christianity Today*, November 21, 2011, http://www.christianitytoday.com/ct/2011/novemberweb-only/gospeljimhenson.html.

5. Robert Jones, "Jim Henson—a Noble Soul," Infinite Fire, May 15, 2015, http://infinitefire.org/info/jim-henson-a-noble-soul/.

6. E. L. Seeley, ed. and trans., *Stories of the Italian Artists from Vasari* (London: Chatto & Windus; New York: Duffield & Co., 1908), 43–44.

7. Jon W. Miller with Mark Hyman, *Confessions of a Baseball Purist: What's Right, and Wrong, with Baseball, as Seen from the Best Seat in the House* (Baltimore: Johns Hopkins University Press, 2000), 171–72.

8. Murray Chass, "Ripken's Last Hurdle Is His Toughest," *New York Times*, May 13, 1999, http://www.nytimes.com/1999/05/13/sports/baseball-ripken-s-last-hurdle-is-his-toughest.html.

9. Cal Ripken Sr., *The Ripken Way: A Manual for Baseball and Life* (New York: Diversion Books, 1999), Kindle ed., foreword.

10. Jerry Kramer, interview, "The Iceman Cometh: Jerry Kramer on the Allure and Lore of the Green Bay Packers," *Idaho Mountain Express and Guide*, September 10, 2004, http://archives.mtexpress.com/index2.php?ID=10229&var_Year=2004&var_Month=09&var_Day=10#.

11. Vince Lombardi Jr., *What It Takes to Be #1* (New York: McGraw-Hill, 2003), 102.

12. Ibid.

13. Larry Page, "The Best Advice I Ever Got," *Fortune*, April 30, 2008, http://money.cnn.com/galleries/2008/fortune/0804/gallery.bestadvice.fortune/2.html.

14. Peter G. Peterson, "The Best Advice I Ever Got," *Fortune*, April 30, 2008, http://money.cnn.com/galleries/2008/fortune/0804/gallery.bestadvice.fortune/3.html.

15. Walker Percy, *The Last Gentleman: A Novel* (New York: Picador, 1999), 4.

16. Carmine Gallo, "Steve Jobs: Get Rid of the Crappy Stuff," *Forbes*, May 16, 2011, http://www.forbes.com/sites/carminegallo/2011/05/16/steve-jobs-get-rid-of-the-crappy-stuff/.

17. Pat Williams, *Extreme Focus: Harnessing the Life-Changing Power to Achieve Your Dreams* (Deerfield Beach, FL: Health Communications, Inc., 2011), 43–44.

18. Andrea Guerra, "The Best Advice I Ever Got," *Fortune*, April 30, 2008, http://money.cnn.com/galleries/2008/fortune/0804/gallery.bestadvice.fortune/22.html.

19. Philippians 3:13, KJV.

20. Neal Gabler, *Walt Disney: The Triumph of the American Imagination* (New York: Random House, 2005), 50.

21. Pat Williams, *How to Be Like Walt: Capturing the Disney Magic Every Day of Your Life* (Deerfield Beach, FL: Health Communications, 2004), 367.

22. Howard E. Green, Amy Boothe Green, *Remembering Walt: Favorite Memories of Walt Disney* (New York: Disney Editions, 1999), 208.

23. Chris Guillebeau, *The Art of Non-Conformity: Set Your Own Rules, Live the Life You Want, and Change the World* (New York: Penguin/Perigee, 2010), Kindle ed.

24. Katie Couric, *The Best Advice I Ever Got: Lessons from Extraordinary Lives* (New York: Random House, 2011), Kindle ed.

25. Coach Bob Starke, "The Great Ones Love to Practice, Prepare," Hoop Thoughts, September 7, 2009, http://hoopthoughts.blogspot.com/2009/09/great-ones-love-to-practice-prepare.html.

26. Faisal Hoque, "What Highly Successful People Know about Perseverance," *Fast Company*, August 7, 2015, http://www.fastcompany.com/3049327/lessons-highly-successful-have-learned-about-perseverance.

27. Lawrence Block, *Telling Lies for Fun and Profit: A Manual for Fiction Writers* (New York: Arbor House, 1981), 74.

Chapter 6 Energized with Confidence

1. Roman Nies, "What a Waste," customer review of *Harry Potter and the Sorcerer's Stone* (Book 1), Amazon.com, March 29, 2013, http://www.amazon.com/review/RSWLMQRKPRLLD.

2. Cynthia Kersey, *Unstoppable: 45 Powerful Stories of Perseverance and Triumph from People Just Like You* (Naperville, IL: Sourcebooks, 1998), 84.

3. Jim Denney, *Muse of Fire: 90 Days of Inspiration for Writers* (Seattle: CreateSpace, 2015), 56–59.

4. Jon Winokur, *Advice to Writers: A Compendium of Quotes, Anecdotes, and Writerly Wisdom from a Dazzling Array of Literary Lights* (New York: Random House, 1999), 46.

5. Farrah Gray, *Reallionaire: Nine Steps to Becoming Rich from the Inside Out* (Deerfield Beach, FL: Health Communications, 2004), vii.

6. Farrah Gray, "What Does It Take to Get There?," FarrahGray.com, December 23, 2014, http://www.farrahgray.com/what-does-it-take-to-get-there/.

7. Margaret Thatcher, "Speech at Kensington Town Hall ('Britain Awake')," January 19, 1976, Margaret Thatcher Foundation, http://www.margaret thatcher.org/document/102939.

8. Michael Jordan with Rick Telander, "My First Time," *ESPN The Magazine*, May 28, 2001, http://espn.go.com/magazine/vol4no11jordanclutch.html.

9. Peter N. Carroll with Yogi Roth and Kristoffer A. Garin, *Win Forever: Live, Work, and Play Like a Champion* (New York: Portfolio/Penguin, 2011), Kindle ed., chap. 22.

10. Mike Krzyzewski with Donald T. Phillips, *Leading with the Heart: Coach K's Successful Strategies for Basketball, Business, and Life* (New York: Warner Books, 2000), 221.

11. Bob Starkey, "The Fundamental C's," *HoopThoughts*, September 25, 2009, http://hoopthoughts.blogspot.com/2009/09/fundamental-cs.html.

12. National Basketball Association, *The Perfect Team: The Best Players, Coach, and GM—Let the Debate Begin!* (New York: Random House, 2006), Kindle ed., chap. 1.

13. Ibid.

14. Seth Godin, "Confidence Is a Choice, Not a Symptom," Seth's Blog, March 16, 2014, http://sethgodin.typepad.com/seths_blog/2014/03/confidence -is-a-choice-not-a-symptom.html.

15. Thomas S. Szasz, *Words to the Wise: A Medical-Philosophical Dictionary* (New Brunswick, NJ: Transaction, 2004), 139.

16. Rich DeVos, *Hope from My Heart: 10 Lessons for Life* (Nashville: Nelson, 2000), 34.

Chapter 7 Multiply Your Success: *The Power of Teamwork*

1. William A. Cohen, *Secrets of Special Ops Leadership: Dare the Impossible—Achieve the Extraordinary* (New York: AMACOM, 2006), 186.

2. Mike Krzyzewski, "Quotes," CoachK.com, September 2006, http://coachk.com/quotes/.

3. Bill Curry, "The Huddle," address to the 2007 American Football Coaches Association Convention, San Antonio, Texas, http://www.afca.com /article/article.php?id=ConHighClips003.

4. Steve Jacobson, *Carrying Jackie's Torch: The Players Who Integrated Baseball—and America* (Chicago: Lawrence Hill Books, 2007), 217.

5. Patrick Lencioni, foreword, in Pat Williams, *Extreme Dreams Depend on Teams* (New York: Center Street/Hachette, 2009), xiii.

6. Robert Barthelemy, *The Sky Is Not the Limit: Breakthrough Leadership* (Boca Raton, FL: St. Lucie Press, 1997), 48.

7. Peter M. Senge, *The Fifth Discipline: The Art & Practice of the Learning Organization* (New York: Doubleday, 2010), 217.

8. Ecclesiastes 4:12, NIV.

9. Meadow's Edge Group, ed., *Quotes from Coach John Wooden: Winning with Principle* (Nashville: B&H, 2013), 153.

10. Bilge Ebiri, "Director Andrew Stanton on His Sci-Fi Fantasy Epic John Carter and Why He's Hoping for a Trilogy," Vulture.com, March 7, 2012, http://www.vulture.com/2012/03/director-andrew-stanton-on-his-sci-fi-fantasy-epic-john-carter-and-why-hes-hoping-for-a-trilogy.html.

11. Susan Cain, "Don't Call Introverted Children 'Shy,'" Time.com, January 26, 2012, http://ideas.time.com/2012/01/26/dont-call-introverted-children-shy/.

12. Jim Korkis, "The Forgotten Brother Who Built a Magic Kingdom," Mouse Planet, March 16, 2011, https://www.mouseplanet.com/9562/The_Forgotten_Brother_Who_Built_a_Magic_Kingdom.

Chapter 8 Guiding Others to Their Success Intersection

1. Charles Webb, "Interview: Actor James Hong On 'Kung Fu Panda: Legends Of Awesomeness,'" MTV.com, November 7, 2011, http://www.mtv.com/news/2623472/interview-actor-james-hong-on-kung-fu-panda-legends-of-awesomeness/.

2. John C. Maxwell, "Questions I Ask Myself as a Leader," Injoy.com, http://www.injoy.com/mis/media/questions.pdf.

3. Susan Forward with Craig Buck, *Toxic Parents: Overcoming Their Hurtful Legacy and Reclaiming Your Life* (New York: Bantam, 2002), 97–99.

4. Alan Fine and Rebecca R. Merrill, *You Already Know How to Be Great: A Simple Way to Remove Interference and Unlock Your Greatest Potential* (New York: Penguin, 2010), 21.

5. Jim Denney, *Muse of Fire: 90 Days of Inspiration for Writers* (Seattle: CreateSpace, 2015), 353–355; Malala Yousafzai, "Malala's Story," Malala.org, https://www.malala.org/malalas-story.

Pat Williams is senior vice president of the NBA's Orlando Magic. He has more than fifty years of professional sports experience, has written dozens of books, including the popular *Coach Wooden* and *Coach Wooden's Greatest Secret*, and is one of America's most sought-after motivational speakers. He lives in Florida. Learn more at www.patwilliams.com.

Jim Denney is a full-time freelance writer with more than one hundred published books to his credit. His collaborative titles include *Reggie White in the Trenches*; *Undefeated*, with Bob and Brian Griese; and numerous books with Pat Williams, including *Go for the Magic*, *Coach Wooden*, and *Coach Wooden's Greatest Secret*.

CONNECT WITH PAT

We would love to hear from you. Please send your comments about this book to Pat Williams:

pwilliams@orlandomagic.com

Pat Williams
c/o Orlando Magic
8701 Maitland Summit Boulevard
Orlando, FL 32810

If you would like to set up a speaking engagement for Pat, please contact his assistant, Andrew Herdliska:

(407) 916-2401
aherdliska@orlandomagic.com

PATWILLIAMS.COM

OrlandoMagicPat